It's My Choice

Soo Myung Chung

ISBN 979-8-88945-111-2 (softcover)
ISBN 979-8-88945-118-1 (hardcover)
ISBN 979-8-88945-112-9 (ebook)

Printed in the United States of America.

Brilliant Books Literary
137 Forest Park Lane Thomasville
North Carolina 27360 USA

CONTENTS

PREFACE

This is a journey through doubt, fear, pain, and joy. It's a story of healing self in mind, body, and spirit through **choices** made in a lifetime; a story belonging to anyone; a story without gender, race, or wealth.

It's my choice! I think of the many times I've told myself that and the years it took before I believed it. They're reminders that I own my decisions regardless what the situation is or who tells me what to do.

Today, self-reminders are less frequent because I feel in control of my whole life, not just part of it. Why? Because I have a *free will*, God's gift to each of us. It's a love-gift given freely, unconditionally. It is without strings, enabling me to **choose** my journey, my path.

How did I come to place a high value on **choice**? I think it began when my oldest son, in the fifth or sixth grade in a Catholic school, shared his day's lesson with me. He said, "Mom, did you know that God gave us a free will, that we can do anything we want?" My response was, "Really? I didn't know that."

I don't know why, but that thought made such an impression that it would pop in and out of mind for many years. Free will, huh? What does it mean that no one controls me? Occasionally, something or someone would jog my memory, and there it was again. It seemed like a lifetime before I began to understand what it meant, but I had to go through certain experiences in living before I could accept it as I do now.

Today, it means a lot to me. With *free will,* I have freedom of **choice.** It's a freedom I had never known existed much less had and used daily. It's been a lifetime of learning—to think, to do and to feel. It was through pain I learned, and in learning, experienced change—inner growth.

Who were my teachers? They were my parents, siblings, friends, husband now departed, children, strangers, and that wonderful part of earth, Nature. Did I forget another teacher, the most important one of them all? No, because now I know that I'm the best teacher for me regardless of how many teachers I've had or will have. Why do I say that? Because no one knows how I think or feel, and no one has the information base from which I function and decide. How do I know I'm my best teacher? I've learned from everyone I've come in contact with, but most of all I've learned from the **choices** made to experience how it is to live this life. These are tests I **chose** to place me where I am today. Some of the tests were long and arduous, eliciting so much pain that I almost gave up. In retrospect, it was after years, that I realized pain was necessary for growth.

Wondering why this writing? Is this a catharsis, a purging of my past pains and ills of inner garbage, or is it recognition? I've been through a catharsis and purging and am at peace with myself. I don't have an inner desire for recognition, and besides, this writing may not be a desirable and salable item, so to desire attention through this means is farfetched. My reason? It is time to share these thoughts with others and, perhaps, assist them to **choose** for themselves as they embark on their life's journey.

I've learned through the years that we are responsible for our whole life and make **choices** for ourselves to achieve happiness; that we do not have to place guilt on ourselves or allow others to place it on us; and that we can heal our mind, body and spirit.

Each of us can **choose** to heal our inner selves and allow this healing to manifest through our outer actions. An inner healing brings balance, a whole-ness. Will not our whole-ness affect our Mother Earth? What is this all-important healing? It is **LOVE**, that all- encompassing feeling and energy that heals all wounds, forgives transgressions, elicits cooperation and trust and brings out the best in each of us.

I believe that it is by loving ourselves we can make progress and become better. I believe that our purpose on earth is to become better human beings by recognizing that special light within us—God. To you, reader, God may be the Universal Consciousness, Allah, or the Almighty. Whichever it is, remember it *is* **<u>your</u> choice!**

I

A SAD TIME

$\mathcal{T}$he alarm rang loudly, too loudly, I thought, as I pulled my tired body from the bed and shuffled to take a shower and brush my teeth.

Bud, my husband, got up too and went downstairs. While brushing my teeth, I remembered it was Wednesday, horseracing day. Damn!

My gut feeling told me he was taking a half-day off from work to be there in the afternoon. It was the end of the month, January 31—his payday. I felt my anger surfacing as I saw him losing his whole paycheck again, a frequent happening. That meant bills would be paid late again, including the mortgage. With children, a place to live was my priority.

Damn the tracks, damn the sickness of gambling and damn those who fed off other people's weaknesses! I wished we had never come to Arizona and lived far from the tracks and Las Vegas, another of his haunts. The day was only beginning and already I felt down, locked into a life with no hope for happiness. With a heavy heart, I dressed and went downstairs. Little did I know then that I was causing my unhappiness.

Bud was sitting at the breakfast counter, smoking his usual non-filtered Camel and drinking last night's warmed-over coffee, another sore point with me. I never could persuade him to switch to a milder brand although he knew the risk for lung cancer if he continued. I also felt that coffee left overnight in a metal pot was harmful to the body, and with caffeine stimulating acid production in the stomach, no telling what other harmful reaction could take place.

This was another example of ignorance for the truth that I could not **choose** for another.

With purse in hand, I walked past him without giving him a goodbye kiss. I opened the back sliding door, stepped onto the patio, turned to face him and said, "And don't forget to pay the bills today!" Everything about me was angry—stance, face and voice. I expected a rebuttal but all he did was look at me as though too tired to say anything, an unusual silence. I didn't pursue it because I was tired too and knew arguing resolved nothing.

I closed the sliding door hard, and as it closed with a thud, turned and walked to the car. Even as I started the car, I thought it strange he didn't answer, and while driving to work, I recalled how tired he looked with a dark, grayish coloring—a coloring I hadn't seen before. I brushed that picture aside when I arrived at work.

Work was as a clinical laboratory scientist (medical technologist), at a specialized laboratory in a large Phoenix hospital. I called messenger service to bring the scheduled patients down for their tests, assisted the doctor, monitored patients and did chemical analyses on patients' samples. A part-time technologist assisted, making patient load manageable and allowing quiet time in the afternoon to complete chemical analyses. While completing my work, I recalled how Bud looked in the morning. I felt funny inside, a strange gut feeling that something was wrong with him. My mind lingered on that picture for a few moments then said, "Nah, forget it, he's okay".

That afternoon, our youngest daughter, Sandy, had a dental appointment at the opposite end of the city. She was only six but seemed mature for her age. Sometimes she would make statements unusual for her age that we'd listen, look at each other, and wonder how she knew that, or where did she get that thought? She also kept things honest.

When describing an event or situation, we couldn't deviate or embellish it because she'd say, "Uh, uh, that's not what you said" or how it happened and reiterate verbatim or describe the scene more fully. She had a good memory, wasn't talkative but was observant and could, if she

chose to, articulate her thoughts pretty well. Of the children, I saw her as the most serious and often wondered why she was so different from her siblings. I had been well conditioned by the older children who were high-energy mischievous creators and who often were far ahead of me. I wasn't accustomed to a serious straightforward child but welcomed the change.

As I was paying for her dental service, the phone rang. The receptionist answered and said, "Yes, she's here" then handed the phone to me, saying it's the hospital. My heart sank with questions racing through my mind as I took the phone—who's sick, who's hurt, what happened? I took the phone, said hello and held my breath as I listened to the voice identify the hospital and herself as the emergency room nurse.

When she said, "Bud's here in the emergency room", I thought my son had been in an accident with his motorcycle, but when she finished her sentence "with chest pain", I knew it was my husband. She asked how soon I could get there. I replied, "In fifteen or twenty minutes" but I wasn't really sure if I'd make it in that time. I knew there would be after work traffic, and with Phoenix being a spread--out city, traveling could be slow.

I slowly handed the phone back to the receptionist trying to feel the words, "chest pain", not daring to think the worst. I stood frozen for a moment then turned to my daughter, telling her we had to go to the hospital to see Dad.

I don't remember starting the car, but I do remember driving to the hospital with questions running through my mind "is he going to die, how bad is it, why didn't he have symptoms before, was the pain under his left shoulder blade two days ago a sign? I told him to go to the doctor, but he wanted to wait until his doctor's appointment tomorrow."

He had hurt his back sneezing two weeks ago, but he seemed to be mending and said the prescribed daily heat and ultrasound treatments were helping.

As I drove to the hospital, I remembered our youngest was with me. She was so quiet I had forgotten about her. I glanced at her sitting on the passenger side so straight and proper. I had expected to see a fearful child wondering what was going on, but instead, saw a child's face void of emotion, no fear or tears. I was startled to see such a stoic composure and was puzzled, but then she was never one to cry easily. I wondered what she was feeling or thinking, but didn't ask, thinking "She's only six, too young to know or really understand what's happening." Little did I know that children intuitively know what happens. They do have thoughts and feelings but may not know how to express them.

Traffic was moderate and flowing well and my watch said we'd reach the hospital within 20 minutes. When we arrived, I was surprised to see our youngest son, Evan, already there. I asked him how he knew Dad was there then remembered that the doctor he worked for after school was our family physician and friend. His partner was the physician on call that day, and since their office was near the hospital, our son, who can move like lightening when he wants to, was there in no time. He had such a frightened look I wanted to hug him but knew he disliked being treated like a little boy. He asked why I took so long in coming. I studied his face but didn't answer. His mind was on Dad and there was no use telling him that in an emergent situation a short time seemed forever.

We walked into the emergency area, and while he and his sister waited, I went into the office to speak with the nurse. She took me to Bud. His face was pale, devoid of blood, with large beads of perspiration though the room was cool. It was sad to see him without his usual vitality and energy, shoulders drooped, lines on his face deeper than before, so tired and burdened as though carrying the whole world.

I leaned toward him and softly asked, "Hi Dad. Are you having pain?"

He looked at me with eyes half closed and slowly shook his head.

I watched his labored breathing and wondered if the oxygen was really helping. I felt so helpless, that same feeling I have for very ill patients who are close to death.

After a few moments, he opened his eyes as if remembering something and slowly recounted what had happened. He was at the horse track and had ordered his usual beer at the bar. While waiting for the first race to begin, he broke out in a cold sweat followed by difficulty in breathing and chest pain traveling down his left arm. He knew it was his heart and asked the bartender to call the ambulance. The bartender first took it as a joke, but when he saw Bud's face, he quickly made the call.

Hmm—I wasn't called until approximately four-thirty and the call was made before the race began, around one-fifteen. Why the delay? My god, he could've been dead before the ambulance arrived! At that time, ambulance service was a private enterprise and slow response was a frequent complaint. I shuddered, hoping that our family would never need that service again in this city.

Shortly after we had arrived at the hospital, he was transferred to the coronary care unit. When I was allowed to visit him for a few minutes, I was surprised to find the cardiac monitor facing him, but knowing him, he probably had requested it. As a Navy trained medical laboratory technician, he recognized an abnormal electrocardiogram so knew what was happening. It didn't look good, but I still had hope. I asked if he wanted to see the children and he said, "Yes, it may be my last time", an unexpected honesty bringing tears to my eyes. He knew, and my gut feeling told me he was probably right, but I was determined not to cross that bridge until I reached it. There's a time for everything in life and no matter how much we hurry or tarry, when it's time, it will be.

I returned to the waiting room where the children were sitting patiently and quietly and told them that Dad had asked to see them. It was the first time I had seen them sitting quietly each with his or her thoughts. I recalled the numerous times I had to scold or give them the "stink eye" (Hawai'i's local term for a dirty look which said, "behave or you're gonna get it!)", but it wasn't needed this time. It was then I saw that children do know when to be on their best behavior. And they decide that on their own. They make **choices** too, which is *their* free will in action. So, what's the parents' role—as guides, until children can stand on their own two feet. As parents, we think we make all their choices, but we don't. They **choose** for themselves. Think about it.

I walked with them to the room but stayed only a moment because I felt it was their private time with Dad. I remembered the many times before, wishing that they had more special times with him, but time was spent on doing things for selves, everyone with different priorities, no two coinciding at the same time. Family-ness and togetherness were being lost. We were disconnecting ourselves from each other, a process that exists in societies today.

I felt sad that we were so caught up in our own lives we couldn't see how we had drifted apart. Was it too late? I didn't think so, but I wondered why it was during critical moments of impending loss we see clearer as to what's important and what's not. It seems that only then we see the shortness of our Earth time, wishing we could turn time back, we resolve to affect change. It points to not only what I see as our mixed-up priorities, but also to the differing values we **choose** for ourselves. Why do we do what we do? What drives us? Why can't I find answers? Hush, the children are coming.

When they returned to the waiting room, I didn't ask them what was said and no one offered to tell me. That was okay because it was their special time with their dad.

As I waited for the nurse to let me know when I could see him again, the priest from the church nearby arrived to give him last rites, a label no longer used. I waited for a seemingly long time worried that something had happened, and no one had time to tell us. I looked for signs of staff hurrying about but there were none. I was relieved when the priest reappeared. He stopped and spoke with us briefly before leaving.

As I walked to Bud's room, the nurse asked that I wait a few moments to let him rest. The wait seemed endless, but when I was allowed to see him again, his face was one I had never seen before—a picture of profound peace. The tense lines on his face had relaxed, giving way to a serene smile that told me nothing mattered anymore, that he was ready to leave this world. He had made final peace with himself and God.

When he saw me, he smiled and said, "Mummy, I have no more sins." I smiled and said, "That's good Dad," as my eyes filled with tears of happiness at his newfound peace and sadness at his probable short-lived peace.

So many of us seek to have peace within, but where do we find it or how do we achieve such a desirable state? Why does it seem to elude so many of us? It just doesn't seem fair that he should find peace at this point in life. Why couldn't he have had it sooner to enjoy longer? Who **chooses** what we should have and when? We do.

My thoughts went back to the priest, wondering why he was with Bud so long. It dawned on me why—confession. I smiled inwardly as I recalled the many times I coaxed him to attend mass or confession with us, but he always had an excuse—he had to work. Sometimes, I felt he deliberately scheduled himself on weekends just to avoid both.

The only other time I remember when he had to go to confession was after I had decided to convert to Catholicism. To my surprise, the priest quickly made marriage arrangements. After all, I was already more than a few months pregnant. Although a Catholic co-worker told me we were living in sin, it didn't really matter since we had already been married in the Methodist Church a year earlier. There was no sin on my mind, for I felt that God still loved me. The priest scheduled our ceremony on a Saturday. It was, I think, a day of reckoning for Bud because he had to go to confession before marriage rites. It had been, I'm sure, more than ten years since he had been to confession, and I knew he wasn't looking forward to it. When I was finished with confession, I smiled at him and said it was his turn and to remember to tell all. He was in there longer than I had expected and thought, "Wow, he's really baring his soul!" When he emerged from the confessional, I was surprised to see him so calm, not perspiring. Purging has its benefits.

Since then, I never could persuade him to go to confession. Whenever I'd ask him to go, he'd say it was too embarrassing. Whenever he joked about going to the "big casino" in the sky, I'd tell him that his sins were too many for heaven to take him. Again, he was a captive for confession after avoiding it for so many years. It was meant to be. It was time, his time.

Looking at the heart monitor, I saw that a larger portion of his heart was involved. He knew it too, but neither of us said anything. He looked at me apologetically and said, "Mummy, you have to cover the lab on weekends." I nodded and replied, "Yeh, don't worry about that now. I'll take care of it." He knew I disliked weekend call because I had argued against being involved. He relaxed more when I said I would and closed his eyes. I didn't know exactly how I'd take care of something I had never wanted and resented doing but wasn't going to worry about it then. It wasn't time to cross that bridge.

I stayed with him a little longer before joining the children in the waiting room. I was concerned that the youngest had been exceptionally quiet and wanted to be close by to let her know she wasn't alone mom was close by. The doctor arrived soon after and suggested I take the children home, assuring me that he'd call me when needed. I agreed because there was no point in all sitting and waiting, especially since it was almost bedtime for the youngest.

On our way out, we met our physician friend who said, "Pray for a miracle, only a miracle can save him." He didn't have to say that because we already were in silent prayer. I didn't have to ask the children to pray for I knew they would. What he said was a confirmation of what my inner already knew, but my mind had walled it off in its never land of denial.

For a moment, I wished he hadn't been so frank because it chipped at the little hope I had, leaving darkness.

I don't remember exactly what I did when we got home except readying the youngest for bed while silently reciting the rosary. I remember that part because that's when the doctor called, asking me to return to the hospital. I wanted to ask if my husband had died, but didn't have the courage, and instead, told him I was leaving immediately. I grabbed my purse and told the older children I had to return to the hospital.

While driving to the hospital, I recited the rosary again unashamedly begging Mary for a miracle. She had helped me before but this was a very important request. I asked her why she wasn't interceding now. Was his death meant to be? It was. I neither could change nor **choose** anything for another.

The doctor was waiting for me at the nurse's station in the cardiac unit, and as I walked toward him, I saw his solemn face. It took all the energy I had to keep from thinking the worst, wanting to wait until he told me. When I reached him, he said that Bud had arrested and couldn't be revived, a gentler word than died, and I was grateful.

I don't know how long I stood there, trying to feel those final words before I asked to see him. The nurse escorted me to a private room, understandably, into a room away from other patients. As I walked up to him, I saw his still form with a fresh cover sheet. I wondered why the clean sheet when it didn't matter anymore—he was gone. It was probably for appearance, something we often dwell on.

We look to others' approval whether we're doing good or bad, wear masks, and even lie to hide our faults—a facade hiding the real us. We see others play games and forget or can't see that we often play those same games. We really hide self from self. We cannot see or forget that we serve as mirrors to each other, and that we learn from others as well as teach them. What we see in others, we may have been, are, or will be. Is there room for criticism? No—only room for good thoughts given to others. It's a challenging practice, but practice makes perfection—LOVE.

Bud looked asleep with eyes partially open, and his coloring had darkened cyanosis. I reached over with my right hand and slowly closed his eyes. As I did that, it hit me that he was gone, never to be in this world, that the children and I were alone, no father, no husband. I leaned over and placed my head on his chest. I couldn't hold the tears anymore, sobbing until the nurse quietly returned and gently placed her hand on my shoulder. Her touch reminded me where I was as I straightened and left the room for the nurse's station where the doctor waited.

He patiently waited as I wiped the tears then asked me to sign an autopsy consent form. I had observed an autopsy as a medical technologist intern, found it interesting and educational, but didn't want it for Bud. I asked the doctor, with a touch of irritation in my voice because the request made no sense to me, "Why the autopsy when we already know the cause of death?" He explained that although we knew the cause of death, other information may be helpful to the children in the future, so with that in mind, I signed the form.

I thanked the doctor and nursing staff for doing all they could to help Bud and headed down to the lobby where I saw our physician friend and his wife just arriving. Seeing them brought more tears. As he comforted me, I thought of the children waiting at home, "What am I doing crying when they're at home waiting and wondering?" I straightened myself, inhaled deeply and told him that I had to hurry home to tell the children. My action was sudden and abrupt, and probably surprised him because he studied my face before asking if I wanted something to help me sleep. With tightened lips, I shook my head, saying I didn't need it. He insisted I take it that it would help me, but I refused. There was much to do and a clear head was a must. I knew a sedative would only cloud my mind and make me lethargic.

As I drove home, I kept telling myself, "He's dead! He's dead!" to feel the impact of those harsh words, but there was none. I felt numb. It didn't seem real that it actually happened and so quickly. From his first symptom, he was gone in less than nine hours. Why, just this morning he was alive and well. No, not really well because I did notice his grayish coloring and unusually tired look. No wonder I had that strange, gut feeling. My inner self knew something was wrong, that something would happen, but I had brushed it aside as imagination and not true. I did that often, brushing aside inner feelings, afraid to rely on them, but now trust them and act on them more.

As I parked the car, I dreaded the moment and thought of telling the children, but felt that somehow they knew. When I walked in, all except the youngest were waiting, looking at me with sad eyes, but before I could compose myself, I blurted out, "Dad's dead!" There, it was out— no class and so blunt! Everyone sat quietly except for our third son who left the room for his own.

When I was sixteen, my brother had told me that I was too blunt and needed to be more tactful. He often reminded me to think and consider people's feelings before saying anything and that there was a nicer way to say the same thing. I did try, but my impatience overruled, finding it too long a process and a waste of time. Articulation with tact wasn't my forte, but he was right, I had much to learn.

To say I *tried* leaves the door ajar so I can say I made an earnest attempt, but it didn't work. Trying gives an out to stop further attempts or to soften the blow of failure. On the other hand, to say I **will** do it, and never mind counting the tries, is a definite commitment, a definite can and will do. When I fall, I get up, dust off, and continue in the path I've **chosen.** When I stop getting up, it's time to depart.

The boys didn't say a word or cry, at least in my presence. I knew that they felt men should be strong and that crying was a sign of weakness. My older daughter and I cried, and we didn't care if no one wanted to join us. I wanted our sons to cry too and release their sadness and pain and encouraged it, telling them it was okay, but still no tears, their **choice.**

After the purging effect of tears, I was able to focus on what had to be done: notify relatives, make funeral arrangements, etc. There wasn't any need to notify his workplace because the doctor was a good friend of his employer, and I was certain he already knew. Being early evening in Hawai'i, I called my sister who knew something had happened when her son, who answered, told her I was calling from Phoenix. She told me she leaped over a small fence and ran upstairs to take the call. I was calm and composed before calling, but when she answered, I couldn't speak. The tears started again and the harder I tried to control them, the more my throat tightened. There was no control, and I could only tell her what had happened between sobs. Without hesitation, she told me that she and her husband would fly out right away. I told her no need that I could handle everything, but her mind was set. I was too tired to insist, and besides, I learned when very young not to argue with her. She's small in stature but mighty in spirit and arguing wasn't the course of action to take.

The next morning, when I let the children decide whether to attend school, our youngest son and daughter wanted to go. I was somewhat relieved that the youngest daughter wanted to be in school because I hadn't told her about her dad. I needed more time to think of how to tell her. Throughout the day I kept asking myself, "How does one explain death to a six-year-old?" I didn't have a pat answer then, nor do I have one now, but I feel the how must come from within oneself at that moment i.e. trust oneself to know the how—follow your heart.

To trust oneself is to love oneself, knowing that all answers to questions come when it is time. Loving oneself is the God-love, Allah-love, or Creator-love that manifests in one's thought, word, and deed, a state of oneness with our Creator.

When she came home from school, I asked her to sit down, that I wanted to talk with her. As I've said before, she was a serious six-year-old. She sat down with an impassive look. I studied her face looking for some sign of emotion, but there was none. Spontaneously, I decided to be straightforward with her, my usual approach. Others may criticize my approach, but the only way I'd know it wasn't the best approach was to **choose** to take that risk and find out. I said to her, "Dad won't be with us anymore. He died last night at the hospital." She replied, "I know." She too, **chose** the direct approach, a total surprise to me. I asked, "How did you know?" "I don't know, I just know."

Her inner self knew, telling me that children are highly intuitive, more so than adults. What happens to it when they become adults? It fades. As adults, we place such emphasis on logical, rational reasoning that we push intuition, that inner feeling and knowing, into the deep recesses of young minds. We push it into dormancy until they **choose** to reawaken themselves when adults. But then, there are those who retain and practice it all their lives. Life is a circle, no beginning, no end, as one changes within to another stage, like nature, transforming into something better, balanced, at oneness with the Almighty.

She already knew so what more could I say. I asked if she wanted to go out to play. She did and off she went. Her behavior was most puzzling. I had expected her to cry and feel sad, but there was no reaction. Instead, she seemed unconcerned as though without feeling. This is my child? I, who could be emotional, have a child so matter of fact about something so serious? Why? No answers.

I was concerned then but learned a year later that children her age don't understand the concept of death but grasp it later. I wonder, is that a truth? Perhaps it is children who do know and understand, and adults do not.

Her older brother left for school too, but I found out later from the school counselor that he had missed two days of school. The counselor understood why when I told him what had happened. Where did my son go? In my mind, I saw him sitting somewhere, outdoors, alone with his thoughts. I knew he was going through a great deal of pain and wished I could help. He was his dad's favorite until his little sister was born, and I knew that his behavior problem in school was to get his father's attention. With Dad gone, he must have been feeling a double whammy—no father, no attention. When something bothered him, he preferred solitude, and all my asking or talking couldn't open that communication channel. Perhaps, someday we'll have dialogue so I may know him better.

I kept myself busy with calls to relatives, making funeral arrangements and sorting through Bud's papers. I also notified the Social Security Administration, Veteran's Administration, and called the Naval Reserve Training Center for burial information. The person at the Center who could have helped with decedent's affairs was on leave, and I was surprised to learn that no one else could assist me. Strange that only one person knew how to handle such affairs. All I wanted to know was how to make burial arrangements at the National Cemetery of the Pacific in

Honolulu. Surely there were standard operating procedure manuals as reference but didn't ask. Why bother asking when the person on the line didn't seem helpful, and I wasn't the type to insist. Anyway, further stress would only deplete the little energy I had left for what had to be done.

From that, I learned that a retiree's status changes to last in line. Active- duty affairs always took precedence. After all, they do the fighting, and never mind that the retiree did his fighting before. The lesson learned from that contact was that I had to fend for myself. So be it.

The one helpful suggestion from the Naval Reserve Center was to call Luke Air Force Base for possible assistance. I was grateful for that.

When I did call, asking about making burial arrangements in a national cemetery, I was gruffly told to call the cemetery first to find out if space was available before I made flight arrangements, and that I "just can't send the body there." I didn't get the name, but I recognized his voice as one of our neighbors, a retired Air Force colonel, two townhouses away. Because of his gruff manner, I didn't dare identify myself as his neighbor for fear he would think of me as a dingbat. I hardly knew him, but after that encounter, I didn't want to. It's interesting to note that the military has later adopted Deming's Total Quality Improvement to improve its processes, one of which is customer service.

By the end of that conversation, my stress and hurt level had peaked, and the tears started again. It was a reminder that some of us seemed uncaring. I wondered why or how we get that way. Is it because we can't find our own happiness, so think and act to deprive others too, i.e. if we're unhappy, we want others to be unhappy? Misery loves company, doesn't it? It was another reminder that the name of life's game is balance, oneness with our Creator.

I was tired of calling the various agencies, repeating myself, and although most were very helpful, that last call seemed to be the straw that broke this camel's back. I just wanted to be alone not caring if I ever spoke with another person, or if no one wanted to help, but my inner self, that ever present inner voice said, "Just do it! it's gotta be done." I inhaled deeply and reached for the phone again.

The next call was to the National cemetery in Honolulu, Hawai'i. When I explained to the woman answering why I was calling, she asked me to please hold and connected me to the Superintendent. He was the first and most helpful person in a very frustrating process. He assured me that space was available, but I needed to contact a Honolulu mortuary to receive the body and make burial arrangements. He also informed me that the Phoenix mortuary should have contacted the Honolulu mortuary to finalize all arrangements for me. I told him that I did ask the owner of the mortuary, but he didn't know what had to be done. I was glad for the assistance and relieved that I was finally getting somewhere. As I sighed with relief, knowing that things would go smoothly, I felt the pressure lift from my whole being. I called my eldest brother in Honolulu asking his help in contacting a mortuary in Honolulu. He called his friend at Borthwick's who contacted me within a few minutes. He assured me that all necessary arrangements would be made after I had the flight information. I was deeply grateful for the caring and efficient manner of all involved who helped make those arrangements so quickly.

After all was done, I wondered, "Why am I going through such a hassle? What did I do to deserve this? Is this what I'm to expect from now on? Why?" It was a lesson in living, doing, and standing on my own two feet. No one had told me that life would be easy, so why shouldn't I have the stumbling blocks? I was being taught, and I soon found that the harder the lesson, the greater, deeper, and lasting the learning. It was also a lesson for better understanding and acceptance of life's daily processes.

To understand isn't enough, but to understand and accept makes learning more complete. To accept self and others reduces stress, all self-imposed, and allows us to focus better on our true path. If we can't accept others as they are and get annoyed or angry because they are not as we believe they should be, *we* have the problem, not them. Imposing our personal values on others doesn't make for successful living. Working to make ourselves better makes for successful living, i.e. to love our whole selves, good and bad, enables us to love and accept others as they are. To think the best of others besides helping when we're able allows us to reach oneness with the Almighty.

Following those calls, I recalled telling my husband a few months before he died, that should I predecease him, I wanted to be buried in Hawai'i, at Punchbowl, The National Cemetery of the Pacific. I asked him where he wanted to be buried, and he said wherever I decided. When I told him it would be at Punchbowl, he agreed. I don't know how or why that subject came up for discussion, but did I sense there would be a death? Perhaps. Do we **choose** when we depart? I believe we do.

The next day my sister and brother-in-law arrived from Honolulu. Although I had tried to discourage them from coming, the children and I were glad they did. Their gift of presence gave us support and a knowing that someone cared, and their sense of humor helped alleviate the heavy and sad atmosphere. It was good to be able to smile and laugh during those dark moments, but I also felt guilty for laughing or smiling, thinking that others would think I was being disrespectful to my husband's memory.

Over time, I've come to believe that a day should never pass without at least one smile on one's mind and face, and actively seeking the opportunity to laugh even if it's only at self. Sometimes we get so bogged down in a swamp of problems that we don't see that the sun does shine— within us. We are responsible for our own happiness.

The day came when I had to select a casket. Accompanied by my sister and brother-in-law, I drove to the mortuary and looked at the various models and prices. I didn't know what to expect but found that it's not only expensive to be ill, but also to die. Those prices showed me that everything in life has a price, not always in dollars, and that there's always a sacrifice for whatever we want—time, money, energy, things, and even life. I finally selected, a decent looking and moderately priced casket, and was making scripture service arrangements, when my sister asked if I would be serving coffee and donuts after the service. I told her that I had never attended a Catholic funeral so didn't know what custom people followed. I turned to the owner and asked if he had facilities to serve coffee and donuts. He stepped back, aghast with eyeballs ready to pop out. I thought, "Oh, oh wrong question!" As quick his reaction, so too, his recovery, to tell me there was no food serving capability. He asked if we served food at funerals in Hawai'i, and I told him it's an Asian custom to serve food. Friends who come to pay their respects and comfort the family are considered guests and are appreciated for their gift of presence. I thought, "Strange he's surprised by my request. He's Italian, and Bud told me they have a similar custom of serving food at funerals."

On the evening of the service, we arrived early for private viewing of the body, a moment I was dreading. My thoughts traveled to the time I was a sophomore in high school when I viewed a dead person for the first time—a classmate. I recalled her still, thin body and pale, ashen face. I couldn't believe it was really she—looked like her, but she didn't seem real. She had been ill and had missed the beginning of school. When she returned, she was thinner, not well, exhibiting a grayish hue, but she smiled and bubbled with enthusiasm. I marveled at her ability to have endured her experience and still have a sense of humor as she related her surgery and hospital experience. She seemed happy, even after going through so much, that I couldn't help but smile with her and secretly wished I could be like her. Sadly, her stay in school was short. It wasn't long after, we were told she had died. I was stunned, and yet, I remembered my inner feeling when I had last seen her. No matter how much I had tried, I wasn't able to see her as healthy or living longer.

When her funeral service was announced, it was only after persuasion by another classmate, I reluctantly agreed to attend. I felt it didn't matter if I were there because my friend was no longer alive. This was my first funeral, and I had never seen a dead person. Besides, the thought of seeing a friend dead was appalling. At the end of the service, everyone stood up and I wondered why until I saw them walking to the front for last viewing. I thought, "Oh no, I don't wanna see the body", but when I felt a tug at my arm and my friend saying, "let's go", I obeyed, walking slowly while observing her mother overcome with so much grief. It brought tears to my eyes—so much sadness.

Reaching the casket, I was shocked and frightened at what I saw. She was a different person, worse than I had remembered her. It was a considerably thinner person, face sickly white with powder. I didn't want to remember her that way. I was nauseous and wanted to leave right then. It seemed time passed so slowly before we finally got on the bus, the ride home longer than usual, and the fresh air not helping a pounding heart and queasy stomach.

Walking home from the bus stop was quicker than usual, but the rest of that day passed slowly, like a nightmare. I couldn't stop seeing her in my mind. I passed on dinner, feeling nauseous through the evening, and retired early to escape the picture my mind wouldn't let go. I thought that if I fell asleep, it would take that last image of her from my mind, but sleep was difficult. The next day, I knew that the picture I had of her wouldn't do and **chose** to remember her as she was before her illness—vibrant and alive. It was a more beautiful picture committed to memory. I wondered why someone so nice had to die so young. Was it her **choice** too? I believe so, for is that not *free will.*

The anticipation of seeing Bud with a similar sickly white coloring roused that same frightened feeling and required a conscious effort for this parent to set a good example of bravery. So be it. I inhaled deeply, held my breath, and slowly walked to the casket. To my surprise, he looked better than when he was alive. It may sound awful, but that was what I saw. I thought it, but my sister and brother-in-law expressed it.

His face was no longer dark and grayish but had a natural light color with a tinge of rose on his cheeks. He looked peacefully asleep. I was so relieved and slowly exhaled, my body relaxing as I reached to touch him for the last time. I knew that it wouldn't be a frightening sight for the children, especially the youngest.

With an emotionless expression, she appeared unafraid, and without hesitation while holding her brother's hand, saw Dad the last time. Perhaps she seemed unafraid because her brother touched him to say good-bye, thereby showing her it was okay and that she had nothing to fear. I didn't really know, only she knew.

The next morning, it was time for another ritual, funeral mass, with our three sons serving as altar boys. Each of us finds and adheres to a ritual or process in which we find comfort and as a means to cope with living. It was an important part of our grieving process. Serving as altar boys was their farewell gift to Dad and a way to help them grieve.

As I watched them standing near the altar, tall with solemn faces, I wondered what their future held for them, for all of us. Where will we be, and what will we be doing? How will the children be affected, and who will they become? Everything seemed so dark, unforeseeable, unsettled.

Funny how one death can raise so many questions to be answered only when it is time.

A time to be born, a time to live, a time to die; so many times, making life a dynamic process. Sometimes, we think we're standing still, but we're not. Progressing to oneness with our Creator is the name of life's game.

Father Hanley from the boys' school also offered mass with the parish priest. It was a nice surprise, and I was grateful for his thoughtful gift especially for the boys who really liked him. As the school's vice principal and disciplinarian, he had pretty frequent contacts with the oldest son for various infractions of school rules, such as long hair, smoking on campus, or unnecessary discussions with teachers—arguing.

With services over, thoughts were on packing and readying the youngest and me for the trip to Honolulu on the same flight with Bud's body. Although the purpose of our trip was sad, I was less stressed, as I thought of going home again especially knowing that I didn't need a lawyer to settle our affairs. I thought of what the funeral director had asked. He asked if I had contacted a lawyer to help with my affairs. He was being helpful, but instead placed a pebble in our wheel. When I said no, he told me that without a will, all assets would be frozen in probate for a very long time. My worry flag went up because it meant that if I wanted to sell our townhouse, I couldn't until after the legal process was completed. If the process took too long, it would place a crimp on our finances.

In retrospect, he did help by prodding me into action and finding out rather than leaving things to chance. It was research time that paid off, plus I was being taught to stand on my own two feet again. If I didn't go through the learning, it would keep reappearing until I learned.

What a bummer! Everyone knew that lawyers were expensive, and that they even charged for telephone calls. I still remembered how much I was charged for less than a five-minute call. I wondered if a lawyer would charge as much as the funeral parlor, but there was no getting around it because I had to find out what's what. Fortunately, the secretary where I worked recommended one she knew whom she felt was helpful and charged reasonable fees. I made an appointment with him and soon after my answering a few questions, he assured me that for the small amount involved, probate wasn't necessary, and furthermore, as far as he was concerned, my husband had given me all belongings in the house prior to his death. He did advise me to make a will in Hawai'i if I decided to relocate there because of differing State laws. His charge? Nothing.

That interaction changed my biased opinion, but of course, there still are those whose priority is money, not service. It really doesn't matter which service it is, high chargers are everywhere.

A few years ago, because of concern for our minor children, I had asked Bud to make a will, but he wasn't interested. This time, it was imperative I have a will before we left for Honolulu. His sudden death had made me acutely aware of my mortality, and I wasn't about to leave anything to chance. The plane could crash, leaving the children without a guardian, and I didn't like the idea of strangers deciding their fate. For them to be stranded, not knowing, was a frightening thought. Even today, I strongly recommend that parents with young children have a will. With that settled, I turned to another task.

The next step was to notify the creditors holding accounts in his name. When notified of his death, the department stores canceled the charge cards but didn't offer one in my name. It was during that time when women, especially wives, were considered financial non-entities even if they held decent paying jobs. I didn't care if they kept their plastic. I was tired of being in debt and promised myself to live on a cash basis. I saw charge cards as a way to entrap others into debt and keep them there. Even now, students are offered charge cards. Granted, the card is a good marketing tool to attract and retain customers, but in so doing, it encourages a debt-ridden society. It's interesting to note that, today, commercial institutions see wives as another profit source.

I see "Charging it" as a way of life, creating a dependency on the market to make us happy. We depend on it for easy access to goods and services, living the theme of "Buy now, pay later" often buying more than we can afford. I also see the benefit of a charge card as a convenience of paying one monthly bill, all of the balance, but how many of us are disciplined enough to stay within earnings received and not use next week's pay or future income? If we can't practice saving, how can we practice buying only when we have the money in hand? Each has to **choose** for self.

It was through Bud's foresight and planning that all our debts were satisfied upon his death. The credit insurance purchased with the loans was our saving grace. The credit union loan was insured without additional cost, but the finance company charged a high rate, which, to me, was another moneymaking scheme. I grumbled and complained about it, but I couldn't fault him because the children and I reaped the benefit of his **choice**. It seemed strange but nice not to be in debt anymore—freedom from another's control. It was the beginning of my regaining control of my life.

II

QUESTIONS, SOME ANSWERS

*A*fter the youngest and I returned from Hawai'i, I asked the children if they wanted to live with their grandmother in Honolulu. They knew I wanted to move back home, but not if they didn't agree. All except one were willing to move. He had been living with friends before his dad died, but knew he had the option to join us later. The others said yes but I wasn't sure if they really wanted it. I thought that it would be good for them to be close to relatives, near beaches, and nicer climate, but it was less than a year after, I doubted the wisdom of that **choice**.

With that major decision made, it wasn't long before we all settled into the routine of school and work, but it felt different. I sti ll felt a void, that something was missing, and I couldn't understand why. I knew and understood that he was gone, but what was I feeling? I did all required of me at work and home. We ate out often because I no longer wanted to prepare meals, and grocery shopping had become an unimportant, dull, unwanted chore. I had to remind myself to snap out of it, the family needed care. Did they? I wasn't sure of anything anymore. True, I was the living parent tending to everything, but did they really need me? All except the youngest were teenagers, a time when they knew it all, creating challenges that sometimes made me feel inadequate and ineffective. I wondered if other parents had the same feeling. Solo conversations were frequent to bring me back to the living.

It was my inner gut feeling, intuition, which always seemed to move to the forefront when I needed it most. It wasn't difficult because I spent a lot of time reflecting on what was, is, or will be. It never failed to bring me back to stand with stronger legs and reminded me to care. It still does. I like to think of that inner feeling as having a direct line with heaven, that perfect place, and my Creator. I wondered, can heaven be on Earth too? Why not? After all, with God, Allah, or the Universal Consciousness *all* is possible.

Work helped fill the void, and I was grateful for it. It occupied my mind to keep me from thinking of what had happened, and from confronting a future for which I wasn't prepared. It wasn't time for confrontation. As a working wife and mother, the only future I had thought of was the children growing up, college, out on their own, followed by our retirement. Thoughts included traveling to other countries, a childhood desire born from family friends telling of their travels. It's an interest, which now includes countries with ancient history.

Why? I'm not sure. Perhaps it's part of my long ago past.

I didn't always want to work. I remembered the many times of wanting to be a stay-at-home mother, spending time with her children until they entered school, but it wasn't meant to be. I had the working mom's guilt of leaving their care to someone else and feeling like a failure when they misbehaved or didn't do well in school. I was always too tired to give them the attention they deserved, but I did take them wherever I went. It was one way of spending time with them. Upon reflection, I think I did that because I thought of myself not them. It was so I could say to others that I took my children places, lessening my guilt. Taking five step- laddered children everywhere, especially shopping, wasn't fun. I was never good at keeping them together as their dad, who demanded obedience, and was usually worn out by the time we got home. I often told myself, "Never again'", but I kept on until their teens when they refused to go with me. Perhaps it was punishment for them too. By their teens I welcomed their company because I didn't have to hold their hands.

Bud often sternly reminded me to hold their hand and emphasized to *never* let go. I still remember the time our number two son, as a two or three-year old, was lost in Sears. I was holding his hand but let go to look at something for what seemed a moment. Bud came to us, saw him gone, and began to show his anger when a woman's voice announced a little lost boy by the name of Mike. Whew, saved by a voice, but I still heard about it all the way home. Time for laryngitis, I thought. That episode didn't cause me to improve, but in a few years, they were older, and a lost child was never a problem. Since then, I've learned that just because there's a problem doesn't mean it'll last forever.

No matter how much I didn't want to work, I realized later that it was meant for me to work. It was just one way for further learning. Working gave me a sense of independence and helped build self- confidence. It made me interact with total strangers through patient contact and taught me the how. It showed me how to work as a team with co-workers. It prodded and encouraged me to better articulate my thoughts and feelings, and further piqued my curiosity to stretch research for learning. It showed me risk-taking, provided a sea of people who were and still are my teachers, and best of all, it gave me **choices**. It was, is, and always will be good for my soul. It makes me good for something. No longer do I think of retiring. Oh, one day I'll retire from my present occupation, but not from life. There are too many things to see, learn, do, and appreciate. Life is a path with many teachers, happenings, and things.

Thoughts moved on to the weekend laboratory coverage that I had promised Bud. He had an agreement with a small community hospital to provide forty-eight-hour weekend and holiday coverage for a fixed daily rate because the day technicians were getting burnt out. This was in addition to his regular lab job elsewhere which included night calls. I foresaw coverage conflicts and didn't want him to take it, but he insisted scheduling would go well because he knew others were willing to work for extra money. I resented the arrangement because I knew that eventually I'd be involved, and one full-time job plus caring for a home and five young children were all I could handle. There were times I felt I couldn't handle them adequately, and in this case, more wasn't better. Well, what I thought came to be when I had to cover six consecutive weekends—a self-fulfilling prophecy. Tired? Definitely, bitchy tired!

I called the medical technologist supervisor, informing her I wanted to relinquish weekend coverage. She understood and said the day techs had already discussed taking over if I wanted to bow out. They now were willing to take it over. Later, I heard that they were willing to resume weekend work because of the higher per diem pay. I could have used the additional income, but the last coverage experience left a bitter feeling. I didn't feel the money was worth the stress. Anyway, as the remaining parent, it was time to place health as highest priority. Feeling tired and irritable from long work hours wasn't my idea of living, and contrary to an older brother's belief, I wasn't mercenary.

Money has never been my god. I like to earn, spend, and save it, but it's never been my life's priority. Like many others, I use it for basic needs. I can't take it with me when I die, so why not put it to use. As one economics professor once said, "Money greases the economy." Of course, I **choose** the where, when, and how much to grease our economy.

III

TAKING CARE OF HEALTH

*G*ood health always has been important to me, but with all that had happened, it suddenly became highest priority. It still is today, because without it, I can't do anything. Money buys people, places, and things, but not good health. I, and not another, is responsible for myself.

Over the years, I've seen doctors cut, medicate, and counsel, but today, I don't believe they heal us. They can give us a jumpstart and assist in our healing process with their knowledge, tools and resources, but I believe that the healing energy or force comes from within.

Why do I say that? While working in the hospital, I've seen patients of the similar age, sex, and medical condition undergo the same surgical procedure by the same physician but have different recuperative rates. I often wondered why one patient did better than another, and after a long time, I noted their differences of perception, attitude and belief towards themselves, others, and their environment. Most of those with shorter recoup times were optimistic, confident, and believed they would get well. They were calm and flexible, seeing their situation as an inconvenience to overcome. Those who took longer or died were apprehensive, tense, worried, and uncertain of how they would fare, sometimes expressing death. True, not all who were optimistic did well, possibly because of wearing a facade not really believing in self, i.e. loving self. It was the same for non-surgical patients. Why did some do better than others? What did they have that others didn't? Good genes, optimism, a belief that they will heal? How did they get to that point? So many questions, no answers. Not yet.

I believe that *free will* gives us a **choice** to enable healing of mind, body, and spirit—the whole person. It's the *will* that's *free* to all—a gift from the heavens from the time of our being. With it we can **choose** our path, crooked or straight. **Choice.** How many times have we heard that from former convicts or others who have digressed from their goals in life?

The **choice** is made with a *thought* which, when *believed* i.e. *faith*, becomes—a *thing*. "Thots are things", my favorite thought (and spelling), and *faith* that inner believing which makes it happen. The two are inseparable. Think about it.

As breadwinner, I had to make certain I was in good health, so decided it was time for a physical exam. I had the usual blood tests, urinalysis and electrocardiogram (EKG). Because of EKG changes, I took a stress test which was abnormal, then was referred to a cardiologist who recommended a coronary arteriogram. I wasn't concerned until he recommended the procedure that had some risk. He said it was one half of one percent. He told me I had a heart murmur, nothing to worry about, but felt the positive stress test indicated further work-up. I was stunned. I hadn't experienced chest pain or pressure, numbness, or shortness of breath so couldn't understand why I needed it.

The more I thought about whether I should or shouldn't, the more afraid I was of dying, but instead of facing that head-on, I quickly switched thoughts to my youngest, ""Who'll care for her if I die now? The older ones will be too busy caring for themselves. Please God, she needs me. I can't die now!" I recalled the death risk of the procedure, one half of one percent, and shuddered at the unlucky prospect of being in that one half percent. As quickly as I thought it, I brushed it aside. No point in making things difficult by thinking the worst. Things were bad enough and I didn't want that thought to become a thing.

Did I feel that life was unfair? You bet! When I received no benefit, it was unfair. It was also unfair to the children, especially the youngest.

I smile now when I recall how little I knew then. I didn't know or understand that all processes strive for balance following ups and downs, peaks and valleys, and since life is dynamic, problems do not exist forever. A problem before us is a challenge to do and learn.

Although the risk was small, consenting came only after a great deal of thought. After all, it was my life not the doctor's. If I submitted to the procedure, I'd definitely know if my coronary arteries were clear, but if I didn't, I wouldn't know and could have a heart attack. It was a dilemma but I had to decide. Another question surfaced, "Should I have it in Phoenix or in Honolulu? It's late March and we'll be moving early June." I needed to bounce these questions off someone and my brother in Honolulu seemed like a good **choice**. He wasn't. He was gruff and abrupt, an unexpected demeanor. I was hurt by his manner and had hoped for a little understanding of what I was going through. After all, Bud died just two months ago, and I still felt I was in limbo. What I heard was an unconcerned individual who seemed irritated and bothered by my questions.

That's okay. I learned from that encounter too. As I moved through my hurt, I remembered that that was his usual manner. I realized that's the way he is, and I couldn't change him. I can only change me. So be it. With hurt aside, I could see that the ultimate **choices** in my life had always been and will always be mine. From then on, I **chose** to stand on my own two feet and make all of my decisions. I may ask for another's opinion or consider their suggestion and available options, but the final **choice** will always be mine, not another's. It was another lesson to take charge of my life.

While married, I had played a subordinate role and had forgotten what it was like to stand on my own two feet. I had relinquished control of my life and allowed another to **choose** for me. That relinquishment also was my **choice.** My parents and siblings had taught me to stand on my own while growing up so why not now? Thank you big brother, for that bolt of lightning! It was a good jolt and a push start. It was a fairly quick decision from that inner gut feeling again telling me to stand on my own two feet, not another's. It was a reawakening to take responsibility for my own life, a life that needed much mending.

As a solo, my first major decision was to go through the angiogram in Phoenix. I called the cardiologist who scheduled it for the following month. That allowed time for more pep talking to self so I could get used to the idea of catheters and a foreign substance in my arteries and heart. I kept telling myself all would go well, but that tinge of doubt lingered, a feeling I couldn't shake off. I felt uneasy.

Admission day seemed to appear quickly with routine and uneventful preliminary testing. I felt like canceling out, but knew I wouldn't because making a decision or choice is a commitment requiring follow through. Any change would depend on additional information or a strong gut feeling to change. Once settled in for the night, sleep was uneventful.

The next morning, I was wheeled into the procedure room where the nurse explained that the injected material would feel warm, and that I was to cough when instructed to push it quickly from the heart. She didn't have to repeat herself for I had already decided to fully cooperate to hasten the process and better my chances for survival. The unknown was scary and risky, as it usually is, but the most frightening thought was that I wouldn't be my own navigator. When I signed that consent form, I had **chosen** to relinquish control. I prayed, "Most Sacred Heart of Jesus, Holy Mary, please guide these people and be with me."

They transferred me to the X-ray table with a narrow table length cradle, which pivoted side to side. I barely fit into the cradle and wondered how they accommodated a larger person. I looked around the room, and saw the video screen on my left, which I watched during the procedure. There were four people capped and gowned in green. The doctor and one nurse were on my right, a nurse on my left and the fourth at the head of the table. There was also a built-in counter behind the doctor and nurse.

It was time to begin. I felt a slight pain when the needle punctured my leg and heard them ready the dye. As the nurse had explained, it felt warm in my chest as though I had swallowed warm liquid. When instructed to cough, I did. The procedure was going smoothly as I watched my heart, which looked like a fat, squatty apple, pump rhythmically on the monitor. After a short time, I felt fluttering in my chest and heard the nurse count aloud. After what seemed like long minutes, they turned me facing right. My mouth was dry and I felt nauseous. I was about to let the doctor know, when I lost consciousness. I found myself floating above a room, looking through a doorway and down at four capped and gowned persons working at a long table. Two were on the right, one on the left, and the fourth at the head of the table. I heard their low, muffled voices as they worked. One person on the right turned to get something from the built-in counter. At that point, I wanted very much to see what or whom they were working on and struggled to hurry closer. No matter how hard I tried to move faster, I couldn't. My movement and those of others were in slow motion, so had to resign myself to slowly float downward while watching the scene with intense interest. At last, I moved closer, just past a doorway, when I heard a woman's voice faintly calling, "Soo." It sounded so far away, I ignored it and continued downward. The voice called again sounding a little louder, and a third time, even louder. I was getting annoyed at the interruption, which drew my attention from the scene below. I wondered who was calling and why, wishing she'd stop and leave me alone, but the voice was persistent. She called again with her voice loud enough to pull me back to consciousness in a sudden, abrupt manner.

When I opened my eyes, the nurse on the left was shaking my shoulder. She asked if I was okay, to which I barely had the strength to nod yes. I felt I had been in a deep sleep with eyelids too heavy to open. My body felt heavy and so weak that I could hardly speak. I was puzzled. Why do I feel so weak, why did I fall asleep when I didn't feel sleepy, and why so heavily? Strange.

I told them I was about to let them know I felt nauseous but must have passed out because I was dreaming a strange scene. I asked what happened, and it was only after an unusually long pause the person at the head of the table answered in a low, barely audible voice. He hesitatingly told me that they had to bring me back. My spontaneous question was, "I fibrillated and you had to shock me back?" Another slow response, a low and soft yes followed. Getting answers were like pulling teeth. What were they afraid of? Liability? Probably. It certainly seems to be medicine's nemesis today. And my questions—why did I ask those questions without hesitation as though I already knew what had happened and only wanted confirmation? More questions, no answers.

At that point, I was acutely aware of a burning sensation in the center of my chest. I said, "My chest hurts," to which the doctor quickly asked, "Where?" His fast response surprised me. He had heard but **chose** not to answer my other questions, and now he wants a rapid reply. When I told him, "The center of my chest burns," he uttered a relaxed "Oh" and continued. Hmmm, why the lack of concern? I understood later when I found a circular burn mark in the center of my chest. As a physician, his primary concern was that my heart hadn't been affected, but his caring was on temporary hold.

I inhaled deeply wishing he'd hurry before something else happened. As he continued the procedure, my mind replayed what had happened. I knew it! My uneasy gut feeling was right that something would happen, but as usual, I pushed it aside, not trusting it, and **chose** to go against it. I should have listened to my inner self, but how could I when fear stood in the way? I was afraid to follow it for fear of failure, that I would be wrong—again. Why did it happen, and why did I come back? It was so serene, so peaceful, and so very nice that I didn't want to return.

The dye's warmth and instructions to cough interrupted my thoughts. The doctor began asking questions. He asked what I had dreamt. I told him of my looking down on four people working at a long table. He asked if they were shouting, to which I asked, "Why, were you shouting?" No reply. When he asked another question, I became annoyed at his probing and curtly answered, "I don't know." Why the sudden interest in my dream? Whenever I attempted to share a dream with a friend or relative, there was no interest, so why now, from a stranger?

Besides, he didn't have the courtesy or interest in answering my questions.

When it was over, I was one relieved, happy patient being wheeled back to the room. I was very weak, requiring help in sliding over to the bed, but I didn't care because the procedure being over was more important. Once settled, my mind went into instant and prolonged replay. There were many questions. I wondered if my weakness was due to defibrillation, zapping the energy from me. Makes sense. Perhaps they used too much, that less would be more beneficial and not weaken. Why did I pass out, and why the dream if I was fibrillating? Does the brain go into a different state when that happens? I had asked how long I was out and someone said a few seconds. If that's true, why did the dream seem so long, why the slow movement, and why couldn't I move faster? Was I really dreaming, and if not, what was it and why did it happen?

In the midst of questions, the doctor appeared to let me know that nothing was wrong with my heart. He said, "You can do anything you want, have fun, be happy!" Have fun, huh! I was right, nothing was wrong, but I didn't listen to my first gut feeling—again! What if I had died? What would he have said to my children? Sorry kids, your mother's heart was okay, but the procedure killed her?

That cynicism passed quickly. All that mattered was it was over and my heart was okay. Besides, I still was experiencing profound peace. It was a feeling that began with the dream, a feeling words couldn't adequately describe. It was a new and wonderful feeling, an ultimate sense of calm that no person or any situation could disturb or take away. It stayed with me for more than several weeks. I didn't want to return from my experience and was annoyed when being called back. Why should I return, when it was so peaceful there with movement slow and gentle, and time meaningless? I couldn't hurry when I tried, but quickly learned to go with the flow. I kept my focus on the scene below, knowing that I would eventually get there. I can't help but think that it was the ability to focus, which kept me on course—an ability that helps me now. I must have had lots of practice. Perhaps it was my childhood training with many bosses, my siblings, who kept my mind on what was at hand until completion.

IV

CHANGE BEGINS

$\mathcal{T}$he whole experience had a profound effect on me. I became contemplative and reflective on how I had lived my life up to that point. All that I had thought important suddenly tumbled in value. Priorities underwent drastic change, and the questions I had growing up were being answered. I had wondered what peace really meant, why we were born only to die, what was it like to die, and was there such a thing as spirit, soul, or ghosts.

Peace, that nebulous subjective state or experience, a human desire that places all things into perspective had come my way. I slowly learned that peace comes from within myself, that happiness is a product of inner peace, and that inner peace comes from loving myself, not just what I perceive as the good part of me, but also what I see as the bad part. Simply stated, the whole of me—self-acceptance. I may regret undesirable thoughts and actions, but I fully accept them as my responsibility, not blaming anyone, not even myself. Accepting is not blaming. It is taking responsibility for all thoughts, words, and actions and allowing whatever is to be. It is letting go instead of hanging on tenaciously. If I **choose** to change, I will—a decision only I, not another, can make for me. Oh sure,

I've had lots of suggestions from others, but they can't decide for me. If I do as they've decided, then I've **chosen** to allow it.

I saw myself striving for perfection, not understanding its meaning. I'm still learning. I disliked making mistakes, and I didn't like it when others made them, but that wasn't perfection. I see perfection as having love in all I think, say, or do i.e. within myself. It's in loving myself, I'm able to give love to others; it's in understanding and accepting myself, I can do the same for others; and in doing all this, I can reach oneness with my Creator.

My out-of-body experience was a fulfillment of "Thots are things" from a long time ago. Perhaps it began as a child when my aunt died. I wondered what the dead looked like and what it was like to die. Was dying painful and was it the ultimate end? I did not see a dead person until my friend died, but even then, I wondered what it was like to die. By then, I had heard others speak of spirits of the dead and that we should pray for them to progress. I didn't understand that progress meant to grow towards unity with our universe, our Creator's universe.

I wondered where the soul went, and with the teachings of heaven and hell, who sets the rights and wrongs to determine placement? The church's teaching is God decides, but who is or what is God, and would I ever see Him? I felt controlled, and yet, I heard the word "Free" or "Freedom" volleyed about. Our world seemed full of contradictions. Why? We do create our own problems—confusion, chaos, hate, and war.

Growing up I wondered if I could experience death without it being permanent but believed it impossible. I learned it was the finale of life. Many years later I read and heard of others' dying and revival experiences and was intrigued that almost all expressed a peaceful feeling. Well, there I was still living after experiencing a near death episode. I had never thought, much less believed that a childhood thought would bear fruit. "Thots" do become "things".

I now believe we do not die. We depart from our physical bodies and enter the spiritual realm where nothing is hurried and time is of no import. Departing is painless and we needn't be afraid. Our souls are immortal, but we still need prayers to help us adjust to a different dimension. I believe that prayers are messages of love that ultimate, timeless, and boundless key to perfection. I also believe that when someone is in a coma or departed, he or she can hear when we call or speak to them, so you see, God does hear us.

Time is irrelevant in the spiritual realm, but we've made it very important in our physical world. I see time as mankind's illusion. Because of our finiteness, we create time and become its puppets just as we create our problems and let them control us. Someone disagreed with me when I said time is man-made. He pointed out the timing of the sun and moon, which isn't man-made. I had no quick reply then, but after further thought, I still believe that time is man-made. We've created time to program others and ourselves because it's difficult for most of us to deal with nebulous, abstract concepts. It gives us a framework from which we can function and organize our daily activities. We use it as a point of reference for our accomplishments and failures, but we cannot see how it imprisons our creative selves from understanding what living is about. Time, too, is an illusion, mankind's illusion.

Buddhism states that life is an illusion, and to me, that means the universe we live in, which includes the solar and lunar systems. Since life is an illusion, we've created our universe with our thoughts "Thots are things"—a most haunting phrase.

I recalled the gut feeling that something might happen during the arteriogram, and it did. At first, I thought of it as a bad experience, but it wasn't. Experiencing peace was a valuable lesson. I couldn't see it before because I had sought it outside of myself instead of looking within. I **chose** to keep myself too busy with taking care of family, working, and other things that kept me from seeing the peace that was always there. I was too busy to take time out and pull away from the day's happenings and reflect on where I was. Not anymore. Now I take daily time-out, ten, fifteen minutes, or longer to meditate—a must for me. It purges my garbage and renews my spirit, and as it renews my spirit, so too, my mind and body.

Gut feeling, intuition, that knowing when something is or will be without being told, experienced, or seen. I've had that often and I know many have too. When very young, I knew if my father was in a good or bad mood before he reached the door, a knowing, which influenced my behavior. When he was irritable, I behaved, but when he was happy, I asked for things or favors. I loved him dearly and am thankful for the freedom of thought and action he gave me as I grew. He never told me what I could or couldn't do, but my gut feeling did. He always drove me whenever I asked no matter how late and never complained. Later, I realized that he probably preferred it that way and now smile when I recall how he **chose** to drive me—how wise! His inner self knew how to deal with me.

Only once did he show displeasure and that was when I was a junior in high school. It was the morning after I had attended a late movie with other members of a youth club and returned home after one in the morning. The club advisor was with us as chaperone. I had told my mother that I was going to a late movie but purposely didn't say how late. I felt that it was time to assert my independence. Well, the time wasn't right, and I had a feeling I might get into trouble with Dad. Later that morning, Dad called me to his room as I was going out the front door.

His voice was firm and serious. I thought, "Oh, oh, he's mad and I'm gonna get it!" He didn't shout but sternly put me through a third degree. He asked where I was, with whom, were there boys, who drove, and was there a chaperone, his name and occupation. He didn't have to say not to let it happen again because I had decided that soon after he began. From then on Mom was my intermediary, but I made certain a time was given.

As a freshman in college, my logic was I was grown up enough to stay out late, but that ever-present inner feeling told me, perhaps not. I decided to find out as an initiate of the Medical Technology Club. The members had planned a moonlight picnic and had asked me to coordinate the food preparation. The late picnic was to begin sometime after sunset and was to end at two or three in the morning. It was a popular late-night activity at the beach where we ate, played team games, swam, and sat around the fire singing or talking while roasting hot dogs or toasting marshmallows. It was just plain good fun. I was really looking forward to it, my first, but when Dad put me through the same questions, I withdrew. It was a big disappointment because it meant he didn't trust me or I was too young, or both. I wondered when he would treat me as a grownup but was too discouraged to ask. In retrospect, he probably trusted me, but not strangers.

That thought of when was answered the following year when I again decided to try for my first moonlight picnic. This time I gave my mother all the details, in plenty of time, including the time I'd be home— two or three A.M. My thought was to give Dad lots of time to decide if he didn't want me to go. To my surprise, he didn't say anything. It's funny, but I don't remember Dad ever saying a direct yes when giving permission. If he didn't object, it was a yes. I had to check with Mom twice to make certain he didn't say no. I was elated because that meant he had elevated me to adulthood. It meant no more listening to, "Children are to be seen, not heard." I was free at last! It was a case of "Thots are things"—what I had wanted, became, when it was time.

Another gut feeling was the year I felt I should have visited Dad. He was getting older, and although he was in good health, I had a feeling that hung on and wouldn't go away. It was a feeling that told me that I'd better start saving for a summer trip. I mentioned to my husband that I had a feeling I should go home and had started saving. I could have kicked myself for telling him because my gut feeling had said, "don't— he'll gamble it away." A few months before the trip Bud went to Las Vegas and returned with a debt he couldn't repay. He told me that I *had* to help, that there was no one else. I relented only after angrily shouting at him. With a great deal of resentment, I withdrew all of the money for him.

I was deeply hurt by what I saw as his selfishness and asked myself, "Why me, what have I done to deserve this?" Sound familiar?

Dad died that year. I was angry at Bud and blamed him for my not seeing Dad. I knew then that I should have followed my gut feeling and made the trip. Too often I didn't follow those inner feelings and regretted it later.

It seemed that my life was full of disappointments, and that every time I felt things were going smoothly, someone came along and destroyed any hope. All I saw was a lifetime of disappointment and discouragement with no light along the way. Each time it happened, a little more of me died, and yet, I felt I had to keep going because the children were so young. Life just wasn't fair. I always saved for my own vacations which were two weeks every one or two years to visit with family. I always took the youngest and every two or more years took all the children so he wouldn't feel burdened caring for them. He didn't like babysitting. Sometimes I didn't have enough, and he would give me the difference, but sometimes he became so unpleasant before my trip, I almost canceled. We occasionally did day trips and even made a trip with our camper, stopping at various campsites on the way to California. With him being on night call 3-5 days a week, there was little time for pleasure and togetherness.

Going home promised the mental respite and re-energizing I needed to continue coping with whatever problems I perceived in my own home. Indeed, life wasn't fair, but no one told me that life would or had to be fair. I had not learned yet that life is not meant to be fair, but, with its many lessons, is meant to teach. We really do have our pick of lessons, and we do **choose**.

In thinking back, I knew that I could have borrowed the money but didn't want to incur further debt. We had enough debt. I see now that I could have refused to pay his debt and let him take the consequences.

After all, it was *his* **choice,** not mine, to overextend. He had a *free will* to **choose** and, therefore, was responsible for his own actions. No one twisted his arm to do what he did. I also knew that I had prevented myself to see my father. No one twisted my arm either, so that **choice** was *mine.*

Recalling the anger I had lived with, made me realize why I felt I was in limbo after my husband died. With him gone, I had no one to be angry at because my primary target was no more. I could not resent or blame him for my problems, which told me that I was angry with myself not those who **chose** to be nearby. All that anger and resentment had created such stress that, with him gone, it diminished markedly. I had lost interest in everything but had to make an extra effort for the children.

Even meal planning and preparation were centered on his likes and dislikes. It didn't matter whether our relationship was good or bad, the closeness of living and the length of time did impact me. It seems that, only when someone close is gone, we realize their role in our lives, good or bad.

I see anger as a defense mechanism that helped me deal with my hurt. The more I hurt, the angrier I became, and the more I directed that energy toward another. I must have been hurting a lot because I was angry often. Anger and hurt had clouded my mind and prevented me from seeing that I could have stood on my own two feet, not on another's. I had created my own prison and relinquished responsibility for my life. I had prevented self from seeing the frustration of not being able to deal with and solve my problems. Instead, I felt helpless and controlled by others. My anger was really towards self for not confronting and handling my problems. After all, the problems I saw were *my* perceptions, not another's.

When I understood and accepted the why of my anger, I began to let it go. I've learned that by understanding and accepting whatever happens as meant to be, I can let go. It's in letting go I have peace within. Things I can change, I do; those I cannot, I accept, be it temporary or permanent. I cannot change the whole world, but I can change me. I've found that in affecting change in self, I can affect the environment I live in—making a difference. There are times when it's very difficult to accept how people or situations are, but I know that I can help by sending good thoughts to others and self. The challenge comes when I especially dislike what another does. It's hard to be good when you don't feel like it.

I'm still teaching myself to love me more, to see the good in me even if others cannot. I know and accept that my faults and errors are a natural part of progressing and also must remember and accept as others go through the same process. I now **choose** to keep others from pulling me down with criticism, by thought or word and deed, understanding and accepting that they, too, must deal with themselves. Are we so different? I think not, at least not in wanting to be loved, and that begins with self. Aren't we all on the path to reach oneness with our Creator?

As thoughts moved from knowing a person's mood to knowing what could happen, I recalled another time when something did happen, as I feared—a self-fulfilling prophecy. I was in third or fourth grade and was at the carnival with a friend. It was getting dark, a cue to go home. We decided to take a short cut between tents, and, as we started walking, I felt uneasy. I was barefooted, my usual state, except when attending school. Because of prior foot injuries from glass, nails and splinters, I liked being able to see where I stepped. As we made our way between the tents, I felt a blunt object under my right big toe. It felt like a pebble, but when I reached home and washed my feet before going inside, I noticed blood on my foot. There was a cut under my big toe. That blunt object must have been glass, probably a broken soda bottle.

"Thots are things"—a most haunting phrase that still helps me to understand that how and what we think does make a difference. If **we** think failure of another, that person can pick up that negative thought. If he chooses to believe, that "Thot" becomes a "thing"—failure. On the other hand, when we think well of another, that too, can pass over to add to or become a motivating force for success. Good thought can have a Pygmalion effect. No wonder positive thinking is stressed especially for children who carry their hang-ups into adulthood. "Thots are things". I choose what I think and do, and I must choose to think the best of others. This doesn't mean I cannot see when their best isn't being expressed in thought, word, and deed.

V

QUESTIONS, MORE ANSWERS

*S*o many thoughts ran through my head as I reflected on the past. I recalled the weekend and holiday laboratory coverage Bud provided for a small community hospital. That was the coverage he had asked me to take care of when he was stricken. The regular lab crew was getting burnt out with daily twenty-four hour coverage. The hospital administrator was looking for someone to cover the forty-eight hour weekends and all holidays. A friend at the hospital called us and asked if we were interested. I said no but Bud said yes because he knew of others who would be interested in the extra income. He tried to convince me that the workload was minimal, but I was adamant. I told him that caring for a home, five children, and a full-time job were all I could handle. I was not a workaholic. He already was taking night call several times a week in addition to working full days. I saw coverage problems later and had a feeling that I would be drawn in eventually.

He was able to recruit two other lab technicians, but it wasn't too long before he had committed coverage with no tech. Since he was on call at his primary job and couldn't fill in, he asked me to cover that weekend. I grumbled and bitched at him for imposing on me. I resented the imposition and felt trapped because I'd feel guilty for not helping if I refused.

Guilt, I wondered if anyone else felt as I did. It felt lonely standing alone. I have learned that I wasn't the exception, that there are many who place guilt upon themselves and have feelings of anger, frustration, and hurt. I've heard some say they feel good when they make another feel badly or guilty, but I see that as a manifestation of their own frustration in not being able to resolve something within themselves.

That episode reminded me of a childhood where family members helped each other with work responsibilities. As the youngest, I had many bosses—nine or more counting relatives, who always seemed to have tasks for me. Since our family had a strong work ethic, I suppose they felt I shouldn't be idle and had to be good for something. If I grumbled or balked at helping, I was labeled as a lazy, spoiled brat. It was true. As the youngest and Dad's favorite, I was very spoiled, but I never thought myself lazy. I just had a different priority, which no one understood—play first, work later.

Having many bosses nurtured the rebel in me, and I admit that all of them played an important role in bolstering my inner strength. It was using a negative situation as a lesson for a positive outcome. When they told me I couldn't do something, I'd do it anyway, but only if I knew I wouldn't get into trouble with Dad. His word was my law. Through the years when anyone doubted my ability in doing something which I wanted to do, I used that doubt as my driving force to prove to myself I could. It didn't matter if that person didn't see my accomplishment because it was only important to me, so you see, each is his or her best teacher, and change agent.

Covering that weekend brought that same rebellious feeling, with resentment. I wanted so much to say no. Helping someone was training from long ago, but I felt I was doing more than my share of work in and out of the home. Why should I do more and against my will? It's to keep peace and avoid any future complaints and reminders about how I didn't help when badly needed, to do it for the children who didn't ask to be born, and, as a parent, I was responsible for their well- being. I've made my bed, so lie in it; grin and bear it; accept it, there's nothing I can do.

All were jail phrases I used to lock my mind into a pattern of thinking and living with little or no thought of options. I made my bed, my **choice**, but I didn't have to lie in it, again my **choice.** I could grin but **choose** not to bear any undesirable situation. I could **choose** to accept any situation as is or **choose** to change it. **Choices** denote *free will* in action.

At that time, I had convinced myself to stop feeling sorry for self and that a good wife helped her husband. Self-imposed guilt was the norm for me. At first, I helped occasionally, but a short time before he became ill, I had to work six weeks without a break because no one else could cover. I was irritable, tired, burnt out, and packed with a lot of resentment. Anger was my usual mood, and since Bud was usually working, the children became my targets. If they hated me then and wished they could have traded me in for a better mom, I wouldn't have blamed them. I hardly spoke with him, and I didn't want to be bothered with the children. Motherhood had become a burden, and with drugs and birth control pills attracting our children, I seriously considered leaving.

Why stick around when it made me unhappy, but that ever-present conscience, that inner feeling, told me I had to stick around. Why, I didn't know. Now, I do—commitment. It was a commitment I had to finish. I **chose** to be their mother.

What a rude awakening when we discovered marijuana in our son's room. His brother was the informer, and I thought, "Oh good! He doesn't want it around either." Wrong! He, too, became a user and perhaps, a dealer too. I should have searched my son's room when I noticed a steady stream of "friends" who stayed only a few minutes. He used and sold it. I couldn't understand why he needed more money when he had a part-time job and didn't seem to buy a lot of things. We definitely had a tremendous value conflict.

I was very angry with him and his selfish seeking of instant gratification, but before long, that anger turned to panic. How would I dispose of it? The community trash bin was out of the question. Children rummaged through it occasionally, and even if it couldn't be traced to us, I could see tongues wagging. Perhaps the neighbors already knew of our son's activity. After all, like adults, children had their own gossip grapevine. Because of the odor, burning was out of the question especially with a neighbor who wanted to and seemed to know everything going on in our neighborhood. With her, the police would be at our door in no time. Then came a brilliant idea—flush it down the toilet. Quick and easy, I thought, but not so when the dry, small particles required more than several flushes before becoming dedicated sewage.

Another rude awakening was when I discovered birth control pills in our daughter's dresser. I had done the laundry and was putting her clothes away. When I asked her why she had them and where did she obtain them, she told me that she was holding them for a friend. If she was banking on my naiveté and gullibility, she couldn't have **chosen** a better time. Perhaps it's because I wanted so much to believe that she was telling the truth, but the more I thought of her reason, the stronger my feeling that she was lying. Yet, I had to give her the benefit of a doubt because I really didn't know, and if she were really using it, she would have found a better hiding place, or would she? Only she knows. Perhaps, she didn't care if I found it, or perhaps, she wanted me to see what she was doing as a statement that I had no control over her. I was being tested—again, by a young one who wanted her independence.

Their dad was hurt when he found the marijuana. I saw the hurt in his eyes, but he never discussed it. I never asked because I felt it would have been an intrusion upon his deepest feelings. He rarely shared his innermost feelings with me, and the few times I did ask, he said little. He didn't seem too concerned about the birth control pills, but after that discovery, he would call home and ask me to make a phone check on our daughter when she was baby-sitting. Sometimes we argued because I'd refuse to call, telling him I wasn't the Gestapo.

I was deeply hurt when I discovered that our children were no better than others and was ashamed because it mattered to me what others thought of us. I felt their actions were inconsiderate and selfish with goals of instant self-gratification. It was a discovery that told me that I had been viewing the world through colored glass, muddying my vision with what I wanted to believe, not what was.

Other feelings surfaced. I failed as a parent, and perhaps, as a person too. Why me? What did I do to deserve these slaps in the face when I felt that I was doing my best? Since their dad worked most nights, I was with them most of the time and felt responsible for all their actions, placing self-pity, blame, and incompetence on self. I was playing the role of a martyr. I had thought that they had good sense not to cause problems so when my world fell, I fell with it. I didn't want to get up. I thought, "No use in trying when I'm slammed down repeatedly; I'm doing my best and can't give anymore; is this pain my reward for giving; will it ever stop?"—self-pity and martyrdom.

It was just one of the many lessons I had to learn from the children that each of us **chooses** for self. It placed my naiveté sharply into focus, keeping it there for a very long time so I could learn more. Little did I realize that I had **chosen** them to become my second-best teachers just as much as they had **chosen** me to, perhaps, guide them, though I did little of that. I became my worst critic and judge.

My **chosen** martyr's role led me to believe that I was giving my best while my husband and children took advantage of me. I couldn't see the lesson that it wasn't meant for me to control another. I couldn't see that the only control I had was over self. It was a lesson I needed to learn repeatedly with the children as my teachers. My values and expectations didn't coincide or agree with theirs, and the more I tried to impose mine on them, the greater their resistance and my frustration. They weren't about to relinquish control of their lives. *My* **choice** wasn't *their* **choice**.

Their actions provoked a serious assessment of my personal values. I asked myself, "Is it really important what people think of us?" I knew that no matter how well I thought of myself there was someone who wouldn't agree. I've often observed interactions between so called "friends", but when one friend left, the other would make an unkind remark, negating that friendship. Here in Hawai'i, it's called "talking stink" about someone. At first, that kind of behavior puzzled me. Why be so nice and pleasant, giving the impression that you really like them when you really didn't? Why pretend, why not be frank and direct, honest? Why speak of love and compromise that value by your action? So many why's, few answers.

I was puzzled because I grew up in a family where everyone usually told it like it was. Dad set the tone and climate for that environment. He was usually polite and tactful but could be direct when necessary. He wasn't verbally aggressive but spoke with firm conviction. I rarely questioned him simply because his wide interests and keen, retentive mind gave him knowledge on many subjects. Many times, I listened to his reasoning and analysis of a person or situation after careful and incisive thought. He wasn't always correct, and he conceded that fact too. My siblings often told me what they thought of me—a "spoiled brat". That hurt at first, but thanks to them, it served as part of my basis for building inner strength and a tough skin.

While attending college, I discovered that I shouldn't verbalize everything on my mind because some persons were more sensitive than others. Once, when asked for an opinion, I thought I was being asked my true feeling and was so straightforward it made the person cry. It wasn't my intent to hurt, but it did, and I felt badly. It also changed our relationship, placing a distance between us. Subsequently, it was with much conscious effort and through frequent trial and error, I learned the meaning of tact and diplomacy. I still believe and practice the direct approach but have learned to be more considerate of others' feeling.

Why? I am not alone in this world but live with many who teach me how to live this life. We are a global family.

I asked myself, "Where's the children's loyalty to us, our family?" I saw them as not caring when they caused us embarrassment and shame from seeking instant gratification.

Loyalty, a value learned as a child, a value not unique to the Asian culture. I had been taught that my actions as a family member affected the whole family, especially parents, so I should not bring shame or dishonor by undesirable acts. It's the same concept of one rotten apple can spoil the whole barrel. Loyalty also encompassed respect for elders who possessed the wisdom of long experience, and respect and honor for our parents who bore us as fruits. Good fruit indicated good seed, but when the fruit was bad, the same was presumed for the seed.

I tried to make loyalty a part of my own family's basic value of love and respect for one another. I thought I had succeeded, but after what happened, I believed that I failed. I wanted to be perfect. I wanted my family to be perfect, but when I saw our imperfections suddenly exposed, I knew that I had created a facade. I used it to show others we were above reproach, when in truth, we were not. Surely others saw our imperfections, so why pretend we were better than they? If I saw imperfection in others, what made me think only I could see.

I see what *I* **choose**, and others see what *they* **choose**. No matter how hard I try to change their view, the **choice** is still theirs, so why be concerned with how others perceive me. I am what I am, and they are what they are.

I am who I am, but whenever I want to see myself, I look into others who are my mirrors. The many faults I see in them are but a reflection of my own—hate, selfishness, grief, love, beauty, peace, and service. What I see reminds me that I'm no different in these human emotions and characteristics. I'm still an imperfect being striving for perfection—to be filled with unconditional love. What do the mirror images tell me? They're saying that I cannot judge anyone else, for in judging others, I'm judging myself, and in judging self, I'm declaring myself guilty of all that I have rejected. Am I guilty? No, but I am responsible for whatever part I played and the same goes for those who played their parts in that scene.

I don't wonder why we place guilt on ourselves. We've created dichotomies of right or wrong, black or white, love or hate, and thus, create our own problems. We've created conflicting views of all sorts amongst ourselves, but more importantly, within ourselves. They confuse us into thinking that we must **choose** one or the other and place it in our personal value book to become our standard for living. We continue this process until we've molded selves into who and what we are today.

Why must we **choose** one or the other, why not **choose** both and allow them to be? Doesn't each have a right to be here; haven't we created them to serve as our lessons in living? Why must there be a right or wrong, black or white, love or hate, and so on? Why indeed?

I think we **choose** one or the other because we haven't taken the time to listen to ourselves, our inner voices which some call conscience, and which I've labeled gut feeling, intuition. We've been taught and well-conditioned during childhood to see the differences and accept what we've been told. The message learned is—**choose** one or the other, not both. If we **choose** both, I see all dichotomies becoming one—no right or wrong, everything just is. The state of oneness is balance. It dissipates conflict and places us closer to our Creator. It would certainly help our Earth.

VI

ANSWERS CONTINUE

My husband's death was a strong reminder of my mortality, but the out-of-body experience really hit home and made me more acutely aware of how short life is on earth. My life could end any moment. That experience marked the beginning of a more conscious journey through life to search and research who I am, and why I'm here.

I asked myself, "If a total stranger walked up to me and asked, who are you? How would I answer?" My answer came only after some thought, "I'm Soo, a child of God." Friends laughed when I told them that, but I didn't care, it was a start. I had an identity and belonged somewhere. The next questions were, "Why are you here, what's your purpose in life? My god, I don't know why I'm here or what I'm supposed to do." It was that inner feeling that told me I did have a reason for being here, and that everyone has a reason for being here. Other questions came, "What can I do, what will I do, when will I do it, and where or how?" All open-ended questions still provoking thought to stir and strengthen my inner self. They help to discover who I am and what I can do. I've learned that the inner takes care of the outer i.e. a strong inner can take care of any outer adversity. I asked many questions, no answers, but I had a feeling they would come when time.

Meanwhile, I had a family to care for and shipping arrangements had to be made for our household goods. I also had to find a responsible tenant for the townhouse before we moved. I decided not to sell because I didn't know if we would remain in Honolulu. Going home on vacation was one thing but living there permanently would decidedly be different because I had moved from there a long time ago. Every time I visited, its physical face changed so much that I hardly recognized it. Each visit made me feel like a stranger.

Planning a major move involved many decisions—what to take, sell, or give away which mover to select, a longer process than anticipated. It was my first as a solo and involved decision-making I wasn't accustomed doing. When it came to selecting a mover, I worried at first in making the right decision, but let that doubt pass after I signed the contract. Signing meant it was a done deal.

With that taken care of, it was back to the usual daily activities of work, school, cooking, cleaning, washing, etc. I had little spare time and energy. No matter how much I tried time management or delegated tasks to the children, there was little time for family recreation and dialogue, but what I lacked most was enthusiasm. We didn't talk much about our feelings, and I have no excuse for how I was, but now know that all work and no play makes one dull. All work and little or no time for respite, enjoyable respite, had dulled my enthusiasm for living. It was my **choice** to fall into that pattern and I could say I had to do it, that there wasn't anyone else. Perhaps it was true that there was no one else, but it still was my **choice** to do what I did. My *free will* makes me responsible for my whole life, not just part of it.

Sometimes, the children and I did talk about their dad and some of the things he did, or what we did together. As we talked, some of their feelings surfaced and I found myself becoming a better listener. How did I know? I'd reiterate what they said, and when they responded with, "Yeh, that's right or that's the way it was", I knew that not only was I developing listening skills but was beginning to understand them and others better. I also found that the better I understood and accepted myself, the more I understood and accepted others as they were.

Listening helped me to understand that life is made of many puzzles, questions, which require research, a searching again for Truth. It begins with a question—a puzzle, followed by discovery of a puzzle piece—an answer until all the pieces are found and the puzzle completed. Then it's on to the next set of questions until we have pictures, which are somehow interrelated to produce one big picture. As each is completed, it must first be understood and accepted before another is revealed to us.

Finding the pieces can be a long and arduous journey, but to understand is so enlightening that it lifts my spirit when another lesson is learned. It provides the enthusiasm for living.

The youngest rarely talked about her dad, but whenever she did, she'd say, "Him", and if I asked, "Who?" she would say, "You know, him". I thought her reference strange and asked why she didn't say, Dad.

With a serious look she asked, "Are you going to cry if I say it?" Startled, I quickly said, "No, I won't cry. You don't like to see me cry?" She shook her head. That's when I knew that she was affected by the sadness we expressed by word or action. She wanted to avoid any word or action that could possibly cause sadness. Only then did I find how sensitive she was, but I also felt that she was hurting. Again, I assured her that it was okay to say "Dad" that I wouldn't cry, but she never did until college when she was able to release some of her pain.

Her straightforward question was another lesson of many that what I feel, think, or do affects others, whether near or far. Thoughts are energy, energy travels and can be picked up by another, so my thoughts do make a difference. "Thots are things". One example is the mood of hostile crowds where the overpowering thought is to create chaos and death while another is the healing energy from one individual or a group, giving service. It tells me to create and have good thoughts for they do boomerang--karma.

She really was a serious child and seemed to understand more than expected for her age. One day, in response to one of the boys, I said, "Dad's gone, he isn't with us anymore." She quickly said, "Uh huh, he is with us. He's with God and God's everywhere." I couldn't dispute that.

Another lesson learned from one so young—faith, simple and uncomplicated. It reminded me of Christ's teaching that as children we enter heaven.

I could see a finger pointing at me and hear a voice asking, "Where is your faith? You've seen blackness so long, what have you done with the light that was there? Where are you in this life and where are you going?" Where was my faith? I had lost it somewhere along the way and had placed myself in a dungeon, but that gut feeling told me I had to pull myself up back to living. I was being given an opportunity to live and a lantern had been lit to show me the way.

Gifts from his employer, friends, relatives, and my earnings helped us over the three months until Social Security benefits began for the children. The loans were satisfied so I was able to manage our expenses without problems. With my attitude of using cash for purchases, I didn't buy anything unless we really needed it. The most useful tool I used was one question, "Do we really need it?" It was effective for me because it required one answer, yes or no. I still use it today, but not as stringently.

Life insurance proceeds were held back because he had increased it less than two years before. He had **chosen** a policy, which insured the children without further premiums upon his death. The company sent an investigator to make certain there wasn't fraud. He didn't use that term, but I never felt insurance companies enjoyed letting go of money. He interviewed me and requested my signature for medical records and also interviewed the attending physician. Satisfied with the investigation results, the company sent me the check. It was an amount that helped us get settled in Hawai'i.

During the investigation, I was so weary I didn't care if they had decided to keep the money. I knew that I could manage with my earnings, and if needed, the children would help too. It seemed that every time I worried about how I'd pay for a needed expense, money became available. It came through as a bonus, a subtraction error in my checkbook, gift, or whatever. I couldn't ignore the feeling that I was not to expend energy worrying about meeting my obligations. It told me that all things fall into place when it was time. The lesson was faith and patience.

I could see that I was struggling to survive. Survival—an important word for many as it becomes the motivating force behind our actions, causing us to compete with one another. Sometimes, it is to our detriment and sometimes not.

Bud was competing as he lived, but I was too engrossed in my own woes, I couldn't see what he wanted. He wanted to be chief tech, at the top. When he revealed this, his innermost desire, two days before he died, I was stunned by the realization that I didn't know him. He was fighting for his life, his survival, and departed without fulfilling that desire, his dream, and I was of little help.

The realization that I gave him no support or saw his need, placed a guilty load on me. If I had been nicer, more thoughtful, and helped him more, he would have been happier and lived longer. To feel better, I would talk myself out of guilt, but a feeling lingered, and I didn't know the what or why of that feeling.

Survival. We're all striving to survive this life as best we know how. I recalled the private ambulance service for Bud and understood that it, too, was competing to survive. At first, I couldn't understand or accept why people go into a service business and not give good service. Why say they'll do something and not do it well? What was so difficult in doing their best?

I remembered my father telling us that when we do anything, to always do it well. He sometimes grumbled about one of my brothers who didn't do his best in a task. I valued his attention and love, so I learned early to give things my best shot. Of course, my best wasn't always the best in others' eyes, but in my father's eyes, I did no wrong, and that's all that mattered.

Now, I understand the motive of business. Profit is the primary reason, service secondary. Oh sure, customer service is at the forefront, but profit is the bottom line. It's survival, my lesson to see beyond my nose, and broaden my world.

Profit is neither good nor bad, it just is, no more no less. It provides basic necessities—food, shelter, clothing; it encourages creative freedom in any field; it allows others to find their niche in this world and blossom; it chains people to its yoke; and it is a means to attain power over and control of others.

Profit is, but as consumer, it's my **choice** to decide its existence, and as proprietor, to **choose** its use. My *free will* allows the **choice** of what, why, when, where, and how. It's the same for all, because as consumers, we allow profit to exist through our purchases. Each of us makes a difference, collectively forming a tremendous power base. It's awesome! As I began to understand the how and why of business, I saw that the ambulance service was surviving in a competitive world to provide basic needs for its families.

I had begun to merely scratch the surface in discovering who I really was, and now with the door ajar, I knew I had to venture out. No more sticking inside my comfort zone. Bravery didn't prompt me, but I knew that if I didn't begin somewhere, I would never know what I had in me and what I could find out there. It was an inner need, that inner voice which prodded me to search, learn, understand, and accept.

VII

RETURNING TO A CHANGED HAWAI'I

*M*eanwhile, as our move date came close, my thought and energy turned to renting our townhouse and finding temporary quarters for the month before we left Arizona. I was anxious to leave the State and get settled in Honolulu, but when departure day finally arrived, I felt sad. As much as I didn't like the desert environment at first, it did become a part of me.

It was later that I dubbed it my first real training site for living. It was in that State I was given difficult lessons with lasting impressions, rousing me from my dormancy. The lessons were difficult only because I refused to change and wanted others to change for me. I couldn't see that I had to change before I could learn how to live. In learning to live, I discovered where happiness came from—within.

As we boarded the plane and settled into our seats, I was excited with thoughts of settling in Honolulu and how good the change would be for all of us. I thought of myself as doing more fun things, and as I thought of the beaches, mountains, and lush greenery, I was convinced that the children would enjoy living there.

I settled into my seat thinking that I did pretty well making a major move with a family. The process wasn't difficult, and I did learn from it.

I learned the value of obtaining several estimates for services. There was a range of prices amongst the moving companies, a situation that still exists for many goods and services. Some businesses cite higher overhead while others use quality to justify higher prices.

The flight didn't seem long when we arrived at Honolulu International Airport. With the help of relatives, we gathered our luggage and set off for Mom's house. With all of us there, a quiet environment turned into a noisy and active one. Mom, who was confined to bed, didn't mind, but my aunt, Mom's youngest sister-in-law, and her daughter viewed us cautiously. I wondered if they felt our presence was an invasion of their privacy. I saw Auntie observing us and noticed her cautious **choice** of words when she spoke with me. There was a reason.

It was a short time later she had a friend help them move, and that's when she told me they were leaving. It didn't matter if they stayed or left, but it did matter that she didn't have the courtesy of informing me when she made that decision. I was angry, and although she was her own agent, I let her know how I felt. I didn't see her until Mom's funeral two years later. She stood by Mom's casket and cried so much, that my sister-in-law said it was probably because of guilt for not keeping her promise to my dad. She had promised him she'd take care of them for the rest of their lives, the reason Dad sponsored her and her daughter. Perhaps it was true, but if so, it was self-imposed. As I watched her sobbing and my eldest sister comforting her, I wondered if her tears would help purge what she felt. I also thought of how our earlier **choices** can return to haunt or fill us with regret later. Anyway, I hope she has come to terms with herself and is okay Mom had a very short memory. She couldn't remember that Auntie had left and often forgot who I was. Because of her memory lapses, some may say she was senile or perhaps had Alzheimer's, but to me, she was a good person whose most outstanding trait was her ever-present good-naturedness.

I can recall only three times when she was angry—twice with me, and once with her friend. When in grade school, I made the mistake of telling Dad that she had spanked me. He gave her hell but that didn't stop her. She spanked me again, and again, until I stopped tattling. It took three times before I stopped testing her **choice** for consistent and persistent firmness. The third time she was angry with her friend. It was one of those rare occasions when she said much.

She spoke little English, and I spoke little Korean, but we managed to communicate well with each other. My children who spoke only English did too. They all loved her and often went into her bedroom to chat with her while holding her hand as they talked. The conversations were usually brief with her telling them to go. Sometimes, as I kept her company, she'd ask in Korean, "Who was that?" I would tell her my son and she'd say, "Yea, yea, yea", move onto another subject then suddenly ask the same question. Yes, she was forgetful, but her pleasant temperament and cooperative nature made it easier to care for her. She also taught my children some of the problems of the elderly and how to care for them—with love.

Since we had moved in June, there was ample time to register the children in school and orient ourselves to a new environment. It was not new to me, but with so many changes since I had left after college, I didn't feel quite at home as before. I had to re-orient myself to the old streets and refer to the city map for new ones. New buildings not only replaced old ones, which had served as my landmarks, but filled in most of the empty spaces and obscured the ocean view of Waikiki. The beach in Waikiki had lost much of its sand to the sea, and with more pale bodies toasting in the sun than swimming, no longer seemed like a beach. Surfing was in with boards, crowding each other to catch the big one and competing with body surfers for water space.

Tourism had become one of if not the largest industry in the State. There were more people, cars, pollution, and increasing crime. Fast foods were in obvious demand and everywhere. It was not the Hawai'i I knew and loved. Although I had heard others call it progress, I did not see it as beneficial progress.

With more people moving to Hawai'i, land became scarce, and coupled with high demand, home prices escalated to near impossibility for purchase by young families. Scarcity increased demand, increased prices, and increased the work force with both spouses working. It changed family life with busyness of work, sometimes with two or more jobs per person, seeing to the needs of family and home, leaving little time for meaningful respite.

As real estate values rose, so did property taxes. An owner could appeal if he or she proved, with documented fact, that the property value was twenty percent less than the County's valuation. The onus was on the owner. How many owners wanted to take the time and energy to contest government, seeing the process as a no-win situation? Few.

The property tax system is nearly foolproof with county valuations based on sales in the area. If the neighborhood is stable with few sales at high prices, values rose drastically, and so did taxes. I think I've seen my property value decrease once, but on the whole it doesn't. The result is locking owners into higher payments each year.

As property owners, we delude ourselves into believing that, since we've paid for the land, we truly own it. Not so. We pay for its use but cannot take it when we depart. Mother Earth remains while the rest of us come and go. We are but temporary beings on this planet. The land we buy and sell to each other is God's land and cannot be taken as our own. However, it *is* our responsibility to care for it with *love*—perfection. If we abuse our Earth, how can we expect to reap her benefits—food, shelter, natural resources, and her beauty? Think about it.

Pidgin had become a strange language to me. Not hearing or speaking it for years had buried it deep in my mind. It was difficult identifying with locals. How could I identify with them when I no longer understood or spoke their language? I had to listen carefully to re-learn the old words and pick up new ones unique to our Island pidgin. I found myself mentally practicing tones and inflections before speaking.

Thoughts, values, and perceptions also differed from lifetime residents, making me keenly aware of the culture shock and alienation I was experiencing in the land of my birth and youth. Added to that, was the question what State I came from, telling me that locals saw me as a mainland transplant. Culture shock—acculturation, brought a stark realization of how dynamic life is, and how I had maintained a fixed image of the island environment, of life itself. I was learning that, as others move in with their diverse values, changes become inevitable, and that conflicts and or resistance, are companions to change. It also told me that I, too, had changed. I was still learning who I was, and finding myself a stranger in my homeland, giving me a sense of rootlessness, not belonging—a new, not good feeling.

I thought of those who moved to another State and of those who came into our country from other lands. I was certain they had similar feelings, especially those from countries with different languages and customs. I also knew that the process of acculturation would pass in time. The differences I felt were due to life being dynamic, forever moving. It was full of varied experiences with the people I had met and places I had lived in.

Even the weather was different, humid versus dry, quickly tiring me as I did moderate work. I was perspiring more with little effort, and my face broke out with an occasional zit, that undesirable teenage skin problem. A whole year passed before I felt acclimated. The children were no different, having to learn as I did and adapting to the place, weather, and all until they, too, felt more at home.

It seemed odd not to go to out to work. I had to remind myself that I was working, caring for Mom and her rentals. I received a monthly salary as caretaker of Mom and her rentals, thanks to Dad's planning for his and Mom's financial independence.

As I settled into a routine, I came across articles in newspapers and magazines on "widows", a word I still dislike and only occasionally use for myself. I felt it categorized and pigeonholed me into a role of a pathetic, lonely, helpless person. I found that it sometimes elicited unwanted sympathy, making me more determined to be the best I could be in my own way—my own person. I didn't want sympathy or pity. I wanted to be accepted as a person standing on her own two feet. The articles stated that a spouse's death in terms of stress had the highest rating, and therefore, widows and widowers had higher mortality rates. One article also recommended that a decision to move be postponed for at least a year.

I didn't agree with the highest stress because my stress had diminished after his death. It was only after some time had passed, I could see that, indeed, I was stressed. The stress of an uncertain future as to where we would finally settle and what I would do. I was in limbo and couldn't see my direction. Leaving our home in Phoenix gave me a sense of rootlessness, of belonging nowhere, especially since I was living in someone else's home. True, it was my mother's home, but it wasn't mine. I also disagreed then, and still do, with the statement of higher mortality because I felt that I should decide my departure. It's my life and I had no intention of being part of those statistics—at least, not yet. That may have been their conclusion, but this widow still had a lot of living to do—too much to learn and do, so little time. I did, however, and still do, wholeheartedly agree with waiting a year before making a major move or change. A change of scenery or environment doesn't necessarily make one feel better. I see it as a temporary postponement dealing with feelings and keeps one from looking at self—self-confrontation. Considerable time with thought does help to give a better perspective for a major decision.

It was too late for me. I had decided in less than a month and moved in less than five months, a case of what's done is done and can't be undone. Yesterday is gone and can't be relived, tomorrow has yet to come and can't be lived, but today is here and can be lived, so regrets for making that **choice** were unnecessary.

Days were filled with the caring for the children, Mom and her property, and other household tasks taking us quickly through summer. We oriented ourselves to the change in living accommodations, food, and a slower lifestyle. I felt strange not going to work but felt good being home for my youngest when she returned from school. I remembered the times the older ones asked why I couldn't be a stay-at-home mother and was glad it was finally possible. The reason I gave them for working was to help support the family not realizing the burden I had placed on them. Although Bud said I had to work, no one twisted my arm.

Our home environment was more relaxed with relatives frequently visiting with Mom. I thought the children were adjusting well, but gradually noticed that they didn't seem happy. There was nothing obvious to let me know. I just had a funny feeling. They smiled and laughed, but I began to notice they lacked the enthusiasm they had before.

When I spoke with them, one son said that with Dad gone, he wasn't motivated to do well. It was important to him to do well for his father. He longed for his father's love that he felt he never had, and with him gone, he felt cheated. He had a deeply buried, unfulfilled need. He couldn't deal with his hurt yet, but in time I was hopeful he would heal. He didn't care for the school because teachers seemed to spoon feed the students, making things easy and unchallenging. His comparison was the Jesuit school in Phoenix, which, in his mind, was the best. The other son caused a lot of "trouble" according to the school counselor. When I met with the counselor, he told me, "We have good boys here", which inferred that my son wasn't good enough to be there. His statement irritated me, but I knew that I really felt hurt. The school principal was more tactful, but I had the feeling I was being bothersome. At first, he seemed a little tense and uncomfortable, but relaxed and nicer when I told him, I was withdrawing my son from his school.

I had placed the two boys in a Catholic boys' school, which spoke of "family" but did not practice it. Where was family when there was little charity? The message I saw was that they wanted only "good boys" to make their task and lives easier and were unwilling to challenge themselves. To practice Christianity is to see Christ in all. Their attitude belied the church's teaching of love and charity. I was foolish in thinking that all Catholic schools would be the best **choice** for my sons. It was another lesson that clergy are human and also biased, and that I should have done more research before applying.

I saw the good in my son even if the counselor and principal didn't. With his dad gone over a year, I wondered why he was still being disruptive in school. When I asked him what was wrong, he couldn't answer, saying he didn't know. How could he, when he was attempting to deal with his pain, a pain with which we all were attempting to deal.

I'm certain my son felt rejected and so did I. I scolded him for causing so much trouble, told him that he would be attending public school, and asked if he had anything to say. He shook his head.

Like his brothers and sisters, he was feeling a hurt, which he expressed with unacceptable behavior. His actions weren't up to societal standards, and they told me he didn't care anymore. The father he loved dearly was gone forever, and he, too, felt cheated. What was the use of caring about anything or anyone, including himself? I could see that his life's journey would be difficult.

My older daughter was unhappy too and made it clear by her behavior that she would have preferred remaining in Phoenix.

Transferring as a high school senior didn't help her get into cliques formed early in grade school. She seemed to be in a constant dreamy state, not really paying attention to what anyone said especially me. Whenever I spoke with her, I saw her expression change to tuning you out Mom. It was that blank, spacey look which she admitted doing years later. She did find a friend, and at first, I was glad that she had until I found out that her friend had truancy problems. I learned from her friend's mother the many times her daughter didn't go to school, stayed out late, or didn't go home. A couple times she was placed in the girls' detention home. I could relate to what she was going through with her daughter and hoped I didn't have to be that drastic. It was bad enough worrying about my son, and now I had two to watch and worry over. It wasn't long before my daughter went the same route of ignoring the curfew I had set, coming home at two or three in the morning, or staying out overnight. Sometimes, I had the feeling she skipped school, but the school never called. I wondered where she went or what she was doing. When I asked where she had been, answers were always vague, and the attitude I picked up was that she owed me nothing and deserved to do all she **chose**. It never failed that whenever I wanted to know where my children were, I always seemed to get an answer. One time the answer came through a security guard from one of the Waikiki hotels. He had found her wallet with her identification card at the disco and was able to call since we were listed in the phone book. It didn't take much to deduce that the bright lights and fast action of Waikiki attracted her, but what did she do there? I didn't know, but God knew.

Her pain began a long time before her dad died, but she had buried it so deeply within, I wondered if she would ever pull it up and confront it. I saw that she missed having a father who could love her for herself yet felt ambivalent about his death. She seemed to feel sadness at his absence yet relieved that he no longer harassed her.

The eldest son who remained on the mainland had to deal with his feelings too. He had left home no more than six months before his father's death, asserting his freedom from parental control. He had been at odds with his dad prior to leaving home, but their relationship seemed to have improved, a case of absence made the heart grow fonder. I saw him dealing with feelings of loss and guilt too, but he seemed to internalize his feelings, hoping they'd magically disappear. He involved himself with people, places, and things that gave him difficult lessons, but for some reason, I always saw light at the end of his tunnel, and that of his brothers and sisters. Perennial optimist? Sure, why not? Good thoughts definitely help.

A few days after his dad had died, he wrote down how he felt and shared it with me. It was a sharing which brought tears as I, too, felt his pain.

> Sometimes I feel so lonely I feel like I could cry
> Or else I feel like loneliness Will kill me if I try
> My father he just left me
> Amidst this hell and rain
> Without a word he left me
> Alone to feel her pain
> My Jesus He's forgotten me
> But I remember Him
> Where is He now why can't He hear
> My cries of help to Him
> This world she seems so cruel
> Blackened to the core
> It's my turn now to pull the strings
> And even up the score
> What say you now you cruel men
> Who thrive on others' waste?
> You too will eat what you have fed
> Tell me, how does it taste?
> And now, and now an upper hand
> Have I opposed to you
> On your knees and beg me dogs
> Your lives are mine to lose
> It stops not here, nor there, nor there
> It never stops my friend
> On and on and on it goes
> With no such thing as end

I saw pain but felt helpless for I knew that I was part of their problems. I wanted to help them but felt that too much time had passed. I believed that it was too late for me to help. I also knew that *they* had to **choose** to shed their inner garbage to begin the healing process themselves. It was difficult standing by, as though not caring enough, and watching them travel their **chosen** path. I prayed daily that they would be helped up when they stumbled, prodded when they wavered, and yanked back when they deviated, so they could learn from all their experiences.

The youngest did fairly well at school, but her teacher expressed concern because she was so quiet. She asked if my daughter was quiet at home too. I told her not at all and that she talked quite a bit except when her favorite TV program was on and would tell me not to talk to her. My concern was her fear of being alone after her father's death and moving hadn't helped. When she was in school or playing outdoors with friends, she seemed all right, but when she was indoors, she had to know my whereabouts at all times. If I left the room without her knowledge, she'd scream and cry out in panic for me. When she found me, she refused to leave my side. One day she asked me if I was going to die too, and when I told her yes I will die someday, she immediately said, "No! You can't die! I don't want you to die! You have to live a long, long time, okay? You *have* to promise!" It was a response with so much fear, I promised her I would and hoped in my heart I could. Thereafter, she often asked the same question, with my answer the same. Her every asking reminded me that I might not be able to keep that promise. I wondered what would happen if I did die soon, but as soon as I had that thought, I changed the channel. No point in creating worry when I can cross that bridge only when I get to it.

She was always with me when indoors and hardly spoke with anyone, including relatives who visited often. When I was at home, she followed me everywhere with me even to the bathroom. She was always with me when I visited her dad's grave but refused to leave the car. It was more than a year later she decided to leave the car and even asked to place the flowers on his grave, but she still avoided the word Dad. I felt sad and knew that it would be a long time before she could release her grief of losing her father and her fear of death, so I let her stay close to me.

One relative was concerned that she stuck so close and told me that I wasn't helping her by allowing it. I knew by doing so, I could be contributing to her withdrawing into a smaller world, but it was a risk I **chose** to take. When a child, my world was small, but as I grew, it did too. I didn't see any wrong or harm in letting her remain in her world longer because I believed and was confident that when she was ready to venture out, she would. It had to be *her* **choice,** her time, not mine. Her need had to be satisfied before she could stand on her own two feet, and I was optimistic that the risk would be worth the benefit.

She didn't understand the meaning of death, but I knew by her behavior that, she too, was experiencing the pain and void of loss. She seemed void of emotion in the beginning, but as time passed, I discovered how much she had been affected. Whenever I talked with her about Dad, she quickly closed the subject, telling me she didn't want to talk anymore and cried if I continued. She needed someone trustworthy and readily available to provide a stable and secure base, and I knew that building her inner would be a long process. How long it would take was irrelevant because strengthening herself was more important. I also knew that I couldn't do it for her that she had to be responsible for her life and **choose** her place in life. All I had to do was be there for her. It was my risk to be so available and I couldn't foresee the result, but that inner voice told me it would be more detrimental to force her to stand on her own two feet. It wasn't time, but when it was, she would let me know— *her* **choice.**

I was learning that children make their **choices** too, but we adults don't always let them. We may make beginning attempts as guides, but many times end up controlling because their values clash with ours— value conflict. I agree that they need guidance, but so do we. We justify our thoughts and actions for and to them by thinking it's to keep them from harm or strike outs in life but am not certain we're succeeding.

They're intuitive beings acting spontaneously until adult control and conditioning turn them into miniature adults i.e. mirror adults. We don't know *all* the answers, and yet some of us lie to maintain an image, a facade, so is it any wonder why children do the same? We are their closest models. What can we do? We can give them space to grow in and nurture confidence with support in all they do as long as they don't harm themselves and others. But best of all, we can give them and each other love, unconditional love.

I felt ill equipped to care for and nurture my children's spiritual needs, their inner selves, that subjective, nebulous part of us all—soul.

How could I tend to their needs when I was unable to tend to my own? I hadn't discovered yet who I was and couldn't fathom who they were.

How could I when I had darkened my world, losing hope to see light? Oh, I did well in tending to their physical needs but had neglected their inner selves, that important part which enables us to cope and truly live. I had placed my feelings on hold too but couldn't see it, and by putting my feelings on hold, I had withheld my love from them. It was a wonder I was able to see their deep pain.

Sure, I now know I can't apologize for anything I had done because I had **chosen** to focus on materiality, thinking it as more important. My ignorance that my inner gut feelings had to be acknowledged kept me from reassessing and further developing a philosophy in life—my standard for living. I was responsible, not at fault, for that stage of life and future progress. I could remain static and have at times, but things do happen when it's time, sometimes when least expected or wanted.

The lesson learned was tending to my soul, that inner knowing consciousness, for clearer vision to see others and myself as I had never seen before. I saw their pain and lack of self-love, the harm inflicted on selves and others, and the need for healing, self-healing. Many were hard on themselves, being their worst judge and enemy. All were and still are my mirrors today. What I saw in them, I was, had been, or still am. Did I like what I saw or still see, and if not, did or would I affect change? I didn't always like what I saw or still see and, yes, I would affect change no matter how long it takes. I've already invested a lifetime so why stop now to **choose** and *begin*, using lessons learned without regrets.

With important personal decisions made, I began to have an inner calm, allowing my spirit to settle. It made me aware, understand, and accept that my material world was a figment of my imagination—"thots are things". My inner self told me that material pursuit isn't my goal, that it's a by-product of my spirituality, and that whatever I want I could have, if I truly *believe* I will—*faith*. A sincere desire, not tied to greed or malice and a deep inner belief, is the creating force for "thots" to become "things.

VIII

DOUBTS

$\mathcal{T}$here seemed to be one problem after another with the children.

Besides looking after them, caring for Mom and managing her rentals required more of my time, raising my stress level again. I had lost that peaceful feeling from my out-of-body experience and had begun to question the wisdom of my **choice** to move back home. I also began to doubt my ability to prevent problems or cope with them and felt like a failure. It seemed that every time I attempted to understand what was happening and why, something else came up. I felt caught in a whirlwind of human problems, which never ceased, and a seeking of solutions which never appeared.

I kept asking myself, "Why me, what have I done to deserve this?

When does it all end or does it ever end? What am I doing wrong, and why is all this happening now? Why, why?" I prayed daily for help, but none appeared, at least none I could see. I know now that I did receive help because that inner voice kept prodding me on to confront and finish the tests I had **chosen,** a long time ago. Like life, problems come and go, and as life continues, problems do not exist forever.

As days passed, I felt anxious and apprehensive with anticipation, wondering what would happen next. It was as if it was the norm for something to go awry and that I was holding my breath underwater until I came up for air. When nothing happened, I relaxed a bit, wishing smooth sailing would be forever, but I still had the feeling another storm would come.

Since I hadn't heard from the public school my son was attending, I thought that he was attending school and that all was well. After all, he got up daily, left for school with books in hand, and came home when expected which made me think that placing him in a public school was a good decision. Not so. It wasn't long after, I received a notice in the mail that he had been absent a number of days. I can't remember how many, but the number wasn't important.

I was stunned with the realization of how thoroughly I had been fooled and irritated for being so naive and gullible. I had been viewing the world through colored glass, and it was time to replace it with clear glass. I didn't need a high IQ to teach myself to dispel ignorance, but I did need to be alert and aware of what's going on around me—my environment.

"Seek and ye shall find."

What mattered most to me was that my son was living a lie, not only to me, but also more importantly, to himself. I asked myself, "how can I make him see that he's hurting himself more than anyone else?

Damn kid! What's wrong with him? He knew I'd find out eventually so why is he doing this?" When I confronted him, the only reason he could give was that history had no relevance for his future. No matter what I said, I couldn't convince him that all lessons, formal and informal did have relevance in his life. He was history repeating itself because others before him had taken that same path, but like his siblings, he tuned me out.

It was just one of many times I felt I had failed as a parent and sometimes wished parenting classes were available but also knew that, if offered, I wouldn't take it. If I did, it would be admitting that I was incapable and defeated—a failure. I didn't need a bad image and still cared about what others thought of me, us. I believed that people made our reputation and had seen others unnecessarily hurt by untruths, gossip. Wanting so much to succeed without help, I believed that I should and could handle everything in my life. Little did I know that help came from many that shared parts of their lives with me—my teachers.

I didn't know how many days of school he had missed, but I wasn't about to accompany him to class. He was old enough to do that little for himself, and if he **chose** not to, he could take the consequences. I felt that he had to learn to be responsible for his own life, to **choose** his own path. I could say he had to learn because I won't be around to prod or help forever, but that's not a good enough reason. If he **chose** to remain ignorant the rest of his life, it was his loss, but I couldn't stop trying. Although I tried, efforts seemed futile because feelings of anger, frustration, and helplessness always kicked in, making it impossible to reach him.

He remained in school for the rest of that year and part of the next, until one day, he told me that he wanted to drop out. He had spoken with the school counselor who agreed and told him he was mature enough to know what he wanted out of life. As he related the counselor's conversation, I thought, "Is that counselor for real or what?" I wondered if my son was making up that story, but my heart said he was telling the truth. I was sad and deeply hurt by his rejection for education that was valued highly when I was growing up, so with a pained and heavy heart, I signed his release paper. Signing it meant defeat a definite failure as a parent and person.

As I handed it back to him, I told him he had to work full time and pay me room and board. Since he considered himself too grown up for school, he had to work and was not to spend time bumming around. I still felt he had a lot of learning to do and that there was a sacrifice for everything he wanted.

Frankly, with my son not studying, I was surprised he was promoted to the next grade but wasn't surprised that the school didn't discourage him from dropping out. The lack of encouragement from the school counselor told me that the public schools weren't different from private ones by wanting to get rid of problem students. Getting rid of the problem ones made their life easier, but I also knew that avoiding confrontation didn't make them disappear. I don't blame the school or the counselor for my son's **choice** because it was meant to be. He and I had a lot of learning to do and learn we did. I also knew that our public school system, including the counselor, had to learn too. They seemed to have forgotten the purpose of their existence—to teach. Perhaps, they too, felt as helpless as I did in encouraging and assisting students to continue their education, but it also told me challenges weren't welcome. Until we face challenges and work through them, they keep re-appearing, telling us to meet them squarely. Avoidance isn't always beneficial.

His school absenteeism was just one problem and seemed minuscule next to drug abuse. I didn't know how long he had used it, but his brother used it, so why not he? Having two potheads in the family was hellish, and as much as I wanted to hide my head in sand, I could not.

Every time I ignored or rationalized a problem away, hoping it would miraculously disappear, it made no move until I faced it. It was from the children I learned the very difficult lesson that confronting meant resolving problems encountered. They were the creators, and I helped by not listening, seeing, feeling, thinking, or knowing what to do. I neither recognized nor accepted the problem as my own. I had a part in it and took care of it with not always the best solutions, but they were my best then. Responsibility didn't stop with me because they, too, had to recognize and accept their part in that same scene.

With all that was happening, I saw his actions taking him to jail. It did. Someone told the police that he sold pakalolo (Hawaiian for marijuana), and one late afternoon while I was on an errand, they picked him up in front of Mom's house. When I returned, I found his hurriedly scribbled note by the telephone that he was in jail and needed bail. He emphasized the message by underlining that it was "no joke!" I was stunned, staring dumbly at it, but as I began to feel the impact of his message, I became angry. No joke! No kidding! Damn, stupid kid, since when is jail a joke? Bail? How much? Can I write a check, or does it have to be cash? Damn! I should leave him there and teach him a lesson, but would he learn?

I knew that I could not and would not leave him there. I couldn't turn my back and walk away, because I felt it wasn't the right thing to do. I called the police station and found out that cash or a cashier's check was acceptable for bail. As I hung up, I decided cash would be quicker than a cashier's check and suddenly realized that it was close to six p.m. when the bank closed. I grabbed my purse, ran to my car, and quickly drove to the bank. Fortunately, it wasn't busy. Having completed that transaction and while walking out of the bank, I couldn't help but think of how strange that he was picked up on a Friday, the only day during the week the bank stayed open longer. Was luck riding with him even at a time like this? Why? Thoughts and questions were quickly brushed aside as I reached the police station.

By that time, I was very angry, deeply hurt, and ashamed, a familiar feeling, but this time I was also fighting mad. I was mortified having to bail my son out of jail like a criminal because that embarrassment extended to the relatives who cared about him. How dare he do such things without thought for them? I could take the embarrassment, but he didn't have the right to place shame on them. I wasn't concerned about those who saw themselves better than us for their opinions had no value to me.

Hawai'i, the 50th State, is comprised of eight major islands with a unique communication system. There's a saying, "No talk stink" about anybody because someone may be a friend of or a relative of, by blood or marriage, to that person you're talking about and word could get back, creating bad feelings. "Talking stink" could alienate one from potential business opportunities or jobs. It also means that when one does wrong, news travel faster with more information, however distorted, than the media.

On the way to the police station, I knew that people we knew would know what he was involved in and wished so much to be anywhere but there. Before going in, I took a couple deep breaths, as if to lighten the load, and approached the window. I placed the cash onto the counter and told the officer for whom I was posting bail. I didn't dare say he was my son—too ashamed to admit and acknowledge that he was my son—a state of denial.

I now smile when recalling how I had distanced myself. I shouldn't have been concerned with what others thought because perceptions are always of the beholder who **chooses** thoughts regardless of what anyone does, and I cannot change them or the whole world, but I can change myself. Will my world ever come together? As surely as our Creator is, it will. Another lesson learned.

The officer seemed surprised, either at the cash bail, or at this obviously Asian woman posting bail for a non-Asian-looking person. Whichever it was, he repeated my son's name as if to verify my request. He then spoke to another officer, who also turned to look at me as he entered an area separated by bars. I later learned from my son that the officer told him an Oriental woman had posted bail for his release. When my son told him I was his mother, he was surprised. That was nothing new because people often stared at us. I suppose it was due to the non-matching appearance between mother and children. On occasion, the more curious or assertive persons asked if they were mine, so the officer's surprise was just another reminder that eyes don't always see true, and thoughts don't always think true.

I could have left him, or better yet, traded him for a new son, a thought picked up from my youngest, who, when peeved at me, announced that she was going to trade me in for a new mother. It was a solution after the fact, but a viable thought for future reference.

As my son emerged with the officer, I glared at him, using all my energy to keep anger in check until we were out of the building. Once outside, I let him have it all—verbal abuse. I didn't care how he felt as it came pouring out. I didn't feel he deserved tact, diplomacy, or further understanding. I understood and accepted the fact that he was feeling the pain of his father's death and didn't care what happened to him, but in not caring for himself, he didn't care for those around him and was hurting himself and them. I was fighting mad, so mad that I told him if it happened again, he'd rot in jail. As long as he lived with me, he had to abide by my rules, and if he didn't agree, he was free to leave. He knew I meant every word.

I didn't want further imposition of his irresponsibility, and yet, because of his young age, I still felt responsible for him, his actions. I didn't know how to break through the wall he had built around himself and thought of the walls the other children had around themselves.

Would I ever understand what was happening to all of us and why? No answers—it wasn't time.

He was very quiet all the way home until I asked why he was picked up. He told me that he had sold a small amount of pakalolo to someone he didn't know very well but felt uneasy about the transaction. Because he **chose** not to follow his gut feeling, he found himself behind bars. It didn't matter that the informer had actively sought a seller, that was his **choice.** My son caused his own grief. When he said he was going to "Get even", I quickly reminded him that he had **chosen** his circumstances and had no one to blame but himself. He was responsible for his actions and that no one had twisted his arm.

That evening, the staff, where I worked, had planned a cookout at a colleague's home on the other side of the island. I offered to make the Korean barbecue so had to attend. At first, I was thinking of dropping off the marinated beef and returning home, but on second thought, decided I needed and deserved a social break. It was better than dwelling in anger and self-pity at home. I told my son that his sister and I were going to a party, and that he was to stay at home. I asked him if he understood and could I trust him to follow through. He replied with a yes I didn't doubt—call it mother's intuition.

The party was fun, but I had more serious thoughts on my mind like thinking of what to do. As I thought of my son's predicament, I remembered that the hostess's husband was an attorney. I told her about our situation and asked if I could speak with her husband. She told me I should and called him into the kitchen so I could relate what had happened. I asked him if we should seek legal help. He said yes, but before I could ask him for help, his wife urged him to represent us.

When he agreed, I felt relieved and somewhat freed from a burden.

It was a strange day with a strange and weird sequence of events. My son's situation happened on a Friday when banks stayed open longer so I could withdraw money for bail and went to a party at an attorney's home where I received legal advice and assistance. It all seemed to fit together smoothly. On one hand I felt that my prayers were being answered, and on the other, I wondered if all that had happened was due to bad and good luck. The happenings were due to his **choices**, yet he received help. Did he do something right a long time ago to get help when needed? It was another time for why and how, but answers came. I was being taught *faith*, that light along the path, and *patience*, a virtue sought but not practiced often, telling me answers will come in due time and that a problem does not exist forever.

Like Nature, there seems to be timeliness for all happenings—a natural process. Many may not agree, but we don't go beyond our five senses either. It's my sixth sense, intuition, that inner knowing and feeling in my heart which also told me that because there is a problem doesn't mean it will exist forever. As life comes and goes so do problems—a natural process.

Court day came soon enough, a day I was dreading but still had hope that he wouldn't be imprisoned. Because he was underage when it happened, his attorney conferred with the attorney for the court and was able to have it referred to Family Court. I gave a huge sigh of relief as the attorney related the good news. I thought, surely he would be sent to the Boys Detention Home because this was the second time he was in trouble though not for the same reason.

After that episode, it became imperative to penetrate his shield or I would lose him forever. If he were incarcerated, he would die. I didn't want to lose any children that way. It was prayer, a thought that helped me find a way to do whatever I really wanted.

The opportunity arrived when he came home one of the rare nights I was up reading. I don't remember how the talk began, but we talked until three the next morning. It was the first of other talks. I discovered that he was most open with his thoughts and feelings. He wasn't talkative in the sense of chattiness but was honest with his feelings when asked. I knew that by what he said to me it helped him understand himself better. Before he went to bed, he said to me, "You're so smart.

How did you learn all those things?" The "things" he meant was that his father's death was a loss so painful to him, he didn't care what happened to him or anyone else, and that he didn't care if he lived or died for his life had no meaning. It was nearly ten years later, when he was going through a divorce, he revealed that it was painful, but losing his dad was still his most painful experience. Someday, not soon, he too will be able to let go.

In the midst of all that was happening, there were humorous moments though the activity was illegal. Our lives weren't totally dark and dreary. The one I remember well was when he was "attending school".

We had a small garden in the front yard, which my dad had started and I maintained for a time. One day after school, I noticed he stopped at the garden, did something then watered the garden and yard before entering the house. He informed me that he had watered the front, including the garden, his way of telling me I didn't have to tend the garden. I thought the sudden interest and activity most unusual but was glad he was showing interest in more healthy activities. He continued for over a week and I became curious at his prolonged interest. Besides, I had a nagging feeling from the beginning, a cue, to be on guard. To satisfy my curiosity and funny feeling, I decided to check the garden one morning after he had left for school. I stood by the garden and scanned the area, noting the vegetables already there, when my eyes rested on a square foot of newly tilled soil filled with an inch and a half to two-inch pakalolo seedlings.

How did I know what they were? While living in Phoenix, I was with a group of clinical laboratory technologists touring the police laboratory and learned what the plant looked like and its aroma when burned.

Seeing those plump healthy seedlings made my blood boil. I was so angry that if he had been at home, he would have had to listen to me all day, an undesirable punishment. The children never enjoyed listening to a raving mother and would disperse quickly and quietly until I had no listeners. Without him, my anger quickly dissipated as I told myself, "Okay buster, two can play this game. I'll pull every damn seedling, crush them, and leave them here so you can see I know what you're up to. Let's see how you handle *that*!" Anger turned to pleasure as I slowly and methodically pulled every seedling and crushed them in small batches to dry in the sun. I was puzzled as to why he picked an obvious place, our garden, when he knew I tended it periodically. It was as if he didn't care if I found out, that his caring was left by the wayside.

That afternoon, I purposely sat in the living room facing the front window so I could see when he entered the gate. When he entered the gate, and seeing only the top of his head, I saw him turn right towards the garden. There was a noticeable absence of the usual running water and more than a few moments of silence before he reappeared. He paced back and forth by the front steps, stopped, and in a most serious monotone, he called to me, "Mom", I answered, "Yes." He continued, "did you weed the garden today?" "Yes." "You did a good job." "Yes, I know." By then, I was doubled over with silent laughter and had difficulty controlling my voice to mimic his serious monotone. I was glad he did his usual after school of sitting on the porch a while before coming indoors because I needed time to regain my composure.

It was senseless and unnecessary to pursue the matter. I've learned during difficult times that maintaining a sense of humor, even when directed to self, is a must to release stress and as a reminder that life is still worth living. Placing a smile or laughter in our spirit should be a daily practice to maintain our perspective.

I spoke with the other children too, but their short responses and reluctance to talk told me that they weren't ready to share their feelings, at least, not with me. I saw their grief manifested by behavior, which only made me angry. They disregarded curfew, didn't communicate when they'd be late, or didn't do well in school. Their general lack of caring and enthusiasm said they were grieving the loss of their dad and felt a void in their lives too.

I knew and understood that anger was my protective armor whenever I hurt and hadn't accepted my inability to solve problems, but I felt that they, too, were part of the problem and therefore responsible for their actions. I was really angry with myself because I couldn't make them see how they played their part and affected others. Sometimes, no, most times, I felt it a waste of time and energy to talk with them. A rock would have listened better, in silence, and without back talk. Often, I'd ask myself, "Will anything ever penetrate their thick skulls? When will they learn that they live in this world, not alone, but with others? How can I make them see what I see?" Without much help from me they too will learn, becoming their best teachers and fulfilling the circle of life.

I saw things to come from a mother's perspective and intuition. Regardless of how much I attempted to give them the benefit of my sight and experience, including those of others, they turned a deaf ear. Cried out, I shed few tears but was anguished with helplessness, unable to prevent them from falling too hard. I saw the difficulties to come if they continued their **chosen** paths and knew the rewards they sought would be short-lived and unfulfilling.

Not taking formal education seriously meant losing the opportunity to learn with others about life and the world we live in, leaving them in a daze as to what they really did and why. Seeking the glitter of Waikiki, drink, and drugs, for whatever reason, gave immediate self-gratification, but didn't bring them lasting satisfaction with self- happiness. Wanting independence and free of supervision was a noble desire, but it required self-responsibility and a knowing that attaining something meant giving up or sacrificing something else. There is always a sacrifice for anything we want. Their not caring attitude and lack of enthusiasm for living was a manifestation of their grief. Only they could confront and work through it. I couldn't help because I wasn't aware yet of my own grief.

IX

BACK TO SCHOOL

*F*or many years before, I was content having a seven to three- thirty job believing that was all I had to do, but while caring for Mom, I began to think seriously of what I wanted to do with the rest of my life. Perhaps, it was due to the hiatus from laboratory work, I really don't know.

I had considered doing graduate work in clinical laboratory science right after college, but after considerable thought, decided against it for two reasons. One was that my father, who had been retired for several years, had supported my eldest brother in veterinary school and me in college at the same time, and I didn't want to burden him further. The second, equally important, was to keep from possibly causing conflict between a former boyfriend and his current girlfriend. He was studying medicine on the mainland, and I would have been at the same school. I was still very fond of him but wasn't about to be the third party of a committed twosome. I wasn't being noble all I knew was that I wouldn't appreciate that happening to me—call it the "golden rule." Breaking up once was difficult enough I didn't need a preventable problem.

Thinking of returning to school was "Thots are things." That thought of long ago came to the forefront when the children were older, and since I was out of the laboratory field, I had time to think about the future. It was an opportunity to look into what the University of Hawai'i was offering. I considered business, but found it would take longer, so decided to remain in the health field and apply to the School of Public Health. Prior to applying, I sifted through the various programs offered by the school and noted their Public Health Laboratory Program, which was definitely out because I had been in lab long enough. It was time to change.

I felt a need to pull my head out of the sand and explore the world I lived in. I was ignorant of what was happening around me, and my narrowed focus of family and work had dulled my senses and fallowed my brain. Family was and is very important to me and work allowed me to be good for something, but I had neglected other parts of my life. It was time to learn about the rest of my environment and me.

Health administration sounded interesting, but health planning interested me more. I wanted to know how administrators or decision-makers planned and made decisions that affected many people, and what information they used and why, so planning became my **choice**. Having decided, I submitted my application and waited.

Meanwhile, I enrolled in a death and dying seminar offered for the first time at the University and taught by Dr. Mitsuo Aoki. His wife, Lynn, helped with Mom by keeping her company one day a week so I could have respite. When she told me that the course was on confronting one's death, I had a feeling that somehow it would help me with some of the feelings I had, and also let me know if I could handle being a formal student again.

I thought I was over Bud's death, something I kept telling myself.

I couldn't understand the tears and tightened throat whenever friends, who knew him, spoke of him. If I mentioned him first, I was all right and had control over my behavior, but if they spoke first, I had little or no control. It bothered me not knowing why and hoped the seminar would help. I asked my eldest sister to care for Mom while I attended class.

If I hadn't taken Lynn's recommendation, I may not be where I am today. It not only helped to again deal with my mortality, but best of all, it helped me deal with grief, what I was feeling but didn't know. It was only after I had discovered what I was going through, I began to understand the why of the children's behavior—lack of enthusiasm and motivation, problems at school, defying authority. True, the problems must have existed before Bud's death, but they were exacerbated and brought to the forefront after he died.

From the list of suggested readings for the class, the one I liked best was <u>Death and Dying</u> by Elizabeth Kubler-Ross. She identified and explained the different stages one goes through when dying—denial, anger, guilt, bargaining, and final acceptance. She also noted that feelings jumped from one to the other or can be in combination, and that grieving family members experienced similar emotions. Understanding and acceptance is what I learned from her. At last, I began to understand why I felt the way I did, and what the children were going through, opening the door for acceptance of self and others.

It was during one class, when Dr. Aoki spoke of feeling responsible for another's death, which gave me another answer—guilt.

Of course! That's why I choked up when someone else spoke of Bud, not when I spoke of him first because I had control over my words but not over another's. I had received another piece of life's puzzle. On one hand, I felt responsible for his death, the cause of his death—I killed him, and if I had been nicer, he would be alive. On the other, I was relieved that he died because I saw him responsible for my unhappiness and that of the children. I felt relieved, but I also felt tremendous guilt for feeling that way because I saw it as wrong, cold, cruel, and selfish a learned value. To finally know that guilt was what I felt opened the door for healing. Thank you, Dr Aoki!

For me, guilt was a feeling that something was amiss, and I've felt that many times. It was there when I didn't want to do as my mother asked, when I refused to baby-sit, didn't do for another especially when they had no other to ask, received a gift and not returned one in kind, or not given to charity. All were self-imposed because of family and societal dos and don'ts, and I had acted against them. I was so well conditioned by them I didn't know who I had become. When I did follow those values, I thought it was with love, caring, but it wasn't. I did expect something in return—the same thoughtfulness or consideration, and when it didn't materialize, I was angry, hurt, telling self not to do any more favors. I hadn't really learned that love was unconditional giving—from within, without strings, expecting nothing in return, letting go, allowing things to pass.

With shoulders lighter, I was eager to share what I had learned with my children and wanted to help them as I had been helped. I felt as if I would, at last, begin to find myself, my purpose in life, and hoped they would too. When we were together, I started with how I felt, sad yet relieved, and told them it was okay to express it if they felt the same way too. I told them it was an honest feeling that needed acknowledgment without guilt, that Dad **chose** his life, knowing the consequences of his actions, and that we couldn't have changed his mind. The talks helped some, but I saw that much more time had to pass before they would be able to let go, if at all.

Initially, I denied his death and placed myself in a vacuum, a void. Sometimes, I was angry with him for leaving everything for me to handle and to raise a family alone. Feelings jumped back and forth to anger, guilt, denial of guilt, bitterness, and hurt until finally, I began to let go and look forward to a future with hope.

As the seminar came to a close, I began to see clearer where I had been, and while where I was going was unclear, I was hopeful. It was with this hope I could express what I had learned.

Despair, agony, wanting to die
Does everyone go through it at one time of their lives
Do they rise above it with hope before they die
Just before that moment of death? I think so
I feel fortunate in being able to reach
For a reachable hope now, before I die
After a hell of despair, agony, and the death wish
A hell so long in time
That I functioned mechanically yet organized
A lonely hell of isolation
Of many questions—no answers
Of many people—few listeners
Of guilt—no rescue
A hell of my own making
Through my own notions

Of my own foolishness
To lose the hope I once had and am now regaining

When the University informed me that I was to be interviewed by a faculty member, I panicked momentarily, talking to self, "Oh no, what kind of interview? Don't tell me I'm gonna be grilled...what if I don't pass? You applied because you wanted it, so go for it...the worst you'll get is a no, big deal...besides, he's just another person like you." Surprisingly, the interview conducted by Ned W. was straightforward and not as anticipated. He was one of a group of faculty members I am privileged to have known and learned from and for whom I have the greatest respect. After graduation, it saddened me to learn that the school administration didn't retain him, even after our letters of support. I also knew that, like other organizations, the school had its factions and unique political process.

During the interview, he told me he didn't doubt I could manage the academic load but wondered why I **chose** planning instead of continuing in the laboratory field. I hadn't expected the question but managed to tell him that I desired and felt a need to change direction. He seemed to accept my answer and didn't pursue it further. I came out without any clue if I would be accepted, but it didn't matter. I knew that patience would give me an answer. It would be great if accepted, but if not, it wouldn't be the end of my life. Life has a habit of continuing.

Either way, it would be a case of meant to be.

Waiting seemed forever, but it wasn't long before I received an acceptance letter. I was elated at being enrolled in the health-planning program. I eagerly looked forward to the fall session. The other big plus was being awarded a Public Health traineeship for which I hadn't applied. Puzzled when I received the letter from the Dean's Office, I called to make certain that there were no strings attached. I was so happy to even bother asking how or why I was selected. I learned later awards were based on work experience and I had plenty of that.

That spring, before the Fall Session, I registered as an unclassified graduate student for two courses, as a self-test, to see if my brain cells were still functional. I had been out of school for many years and felt compelled to know if I could handle a full-time academic load. The two courses were an undergraduate psychology course and a graduate course on the medical care system, a requirement for health planning. I enjoyed both courses and was relieved to find that I was disciplined enough to keep up with the readings and assignments. My grades were good, and although I would've preferred my grade for the graduate course was as high as the other, I knew I could handle the load.

That positive lesson permitted a mental note to self and which I've said to others, "You're never too old to learn." It's my belief that I can learn until I depart from this life and my **choice** not to allow chronological age to hinder me in that pursuit. When I've said that to others, some said that's impossible because brain cells die daily, but I say, "Use or lose", the same as muscle which must be used or lose its function. Exercise is necessary for our whole being—mind, body, and spirit— balance.

With God, all things are possible, and since I'm from God, why should I allow others to **choose** what or how I think, believe, or do? What is age? It is time. Time is a man-made illusion, and since age is tied to time, it, too, is an illusion—a state of mind. "Thots are things." Focusing on age is a limitation and a hindrance to personal growth. I feel many of us have allowed others to prevent us from truly living when we believe phrases such as, "When you get older, you'll slow down, get sick and can't do as much; you're too old, you shouldn't do that; or old people don't act like that, act your age," etc.

As a child, I often wondered how we were supposed to behave or just be at any age. Our size definitely changed, our vocabulary and thought processes broadened, but these were more related to our physical world. Did our most inner depth i.e. the very inner self change? I think so. Science has studies, which say that we slow down with advancing age, but what makes their data correct? Could not other intangible variables have more impact? I say, yes, they can, for nothing is set in cement. I think we humans give up on living too soon and accept a way of life which tells us we must believe and follow the standards others have developed for us.

We're told the life expectancy of a male and female child born today, of illnesses to expect if we live longer, and of fixed incomes and loneliness when old. These are only some of the conclusions from the many studies mankind delves in. I sometimes wonder if all these studies are really necessary or helpful especially when they counter or dispute another.

When public arguments begin, I wonder if a study's accuracy and helpfulness is the true motive. I've heard and read of studies with recognition and status as the primary motive sometimes accompanied by money. I am a non-expert merely asking questions. I used to take a published study as almost gospel, but now question some because I can't always see the benefits of the study. True, the cited percentages may give us heads up on what could happen and offer ways of preventing the bad or prolonging the good, but as expert information, it can also make us believe we're sicker than we are, which could harm. Where is the happy medium or balance? In self. **Choose** to educate oneself—read, ask, reflect to sift and evaluate, maintaining flexibility and openness to discard the unneeded and acquire the better. Be thy own guide, follow your heart— your intuition. Why focus on dying when we can focus on living? I do not see or believe that living longer means I won't be able to do as I wish because age has not, is not, and will not be my focus in life. Anyway, others will keep track of it for me, and if that makes them happy, so be it. I've **chosen** not to allow anyone, and they're everywhere, to hurry me to the grave, for that, too, will by my **choice**. In taking responsibility for self, I become better, and if need be, assist others.

It seems that many of us, at any age, see or speak of others dying, not ourselves. Is it a manifestation of fear—of death, loss of doing? The young usually see and speak of the old dying, not themselves, and the old speak of their friends, acquaintances dying, occasionally thinking aloud of their time, and then there are those who are quietly ready without fear. How nice to be able to meet that last moment with total acceptance. Mortality and finiteness seem to make a greater impression after a very important and sudden loss of someone or something dear to us. Before then, we forget we're temporary beings on Earth and will someday depart, and that material items do wear out or are lost. Knowing and understanding it isn't hard, but total acceptance is. I thank Dr. Elizabeth Kubler-Ross and Dr. Aoki for showing me that death is a part of life, a departure to a different realm. It doesn't mean I want to die now, heck no, I'm saying it helps me to search and understand why I'm here—my purpose, and when it's time to leave, I wish it to be with total acceptance.

Understanding and accepting death, as part of life is to know my life may end today, this moment. That knowing is a good motivator to do what should be done today not procrastinate and to do my best now, not later, for tomorrow may never come, an opportunity lost. To accept and do even the most boring, trivial and mundane things in life is part of the universe, our world. We are to accept all peoples regardless of race, education, money, position, and power to reach a better state, one which seems to have been lost along the way.

It was with quiet enthusiasm I began at UH Manoa. The first day began with a general assembly, and I sat in the back, listening as I looked over the large group. The age range was surprising, being from mid- twenties to sixties, telling me that times had changed even in the academic setting. More mature people were seeking higher education, a far cry from when I first attended college. Instead of the bright, fresh, young faces, I saw mostly older individuals who looked seriously intent in their purpose. It was one of my first school lessons that as demographics change so do trends and that life, indeed, continues. I could see that by dropping out of life it had passed me without notice, becoming obvious only after I had returned.

The age range wasn't the only surprise. The other was the informal dress of shorts with tee shirts, slippers or thongs, and hair of all styles. Another were backpacks for books, personal items, or whatever, giving relief to sore arms and shoulders and the convenience of free hands, a change I welcomed and still use in my travels. I saw the change saying education was the name of the game, not a dress code—good focus. The external change was good, but my internal still felt uncomfortable being a student again.

In classes and seminars, I listened, observed, and rarely spoke, usual for me when with people I didn't know. I had always been a background person, listening and saying little because I couldn't think of what to say. When in college someone called me an introvert, a new word, an old feeling, but he was right. The why was because I didn't feel intellectually endowed to participate in discussions and was awed by those who could. Those who spoke must have intimidated me, because as I listened, I saw my ignorance of what was out there and couldn't see what was in me. I had a lot of learning and catching up to do.

It seemed others articulated their thoughts and feelings well, and how I wished it for me. I marveled at how they spoke from the top of their heads and wondered what thought processes they used for their various ideas. They made me feel inadequate. Not so, *I* made myself feel that way. They didn't control my feelings, *I* did.

It wasn't until the semester was almost over I began to relax, but only because I knew the students and professors better and was beginning to feel part of the group. It seemed like a long time before I felt the climate trusting enough before taking the risk to speak, provided I had something worthwhile to say. It wasn't unusual to do mental practice before speaking, but my most important discovery was to be natural, be myself.

Inner discussions and frequent reminders to self for oral participation were necessary, prodding me to take the risk. By **choosing** to enter school, I had committed myself to become better—not better than others, but better than I had been. I was on my way to mending and healing myself and "taking risks", which Dr. Bill G and Jerry G often said is a good way to find out how and what to do. In other words, I wouldn't know until I crossed the bridge when I reached it to find out what's beyond. That commitment meant I could no longer sit back, fearful of making mistakes but had to expand my information base to understand myself better. It is in knowing oneself, I can better understand and accept others and the world I live in.

Lack of confidence caused self-consciousness and an unwillingness to participate in discussions. It was a fear that the whole world would see and laugh at my bumbling ways. I felt others like me were everywhere even in school and they were. I was enlightened and relieved when they openly shared their fears because it confirmed what I saw but wasn't sure. The most important lesson was the risk they took to admit their fears to people they hardly knew clearly showing me that no climate was totally "safe" It was another Bill and Jerry lesson, and that if I wanted to make my thoughts and feelings known, then I, too, had to take the risk. Taking risks denotes courage to face unknown consequences, lessons to better self.

Why the fear? Don't really know, but it could be due to being repeatedly put down, not being supported by others, or just the big unknown of not being able to predict or know the result. All reasons may not be known, but the important thing is to focus, and overcome it the best way I know. Regardless of the why, I think it all boils down to not loving ourselves most of all and, secondly, not being loved by others because we spend much time tearing self and others down. As we belittle another in mind, body, and spirit, we do the same to ourselves, forgetting our connectedness, as one *ohana* (Hawaiian for family).

As others shared, it showed me the love they had for others and the love they wanted from others—unconditional love. The message was clear, "accept me without judgment as I wish to accept you." It also taught me the courage many had to **choose** living their lives as they desired, and I certainly needed to do just that—**choose** and act.

The risks I took were speaking more, writing what I really felt and interacting with those I hardly knew. A few told me I should speak more in class. Little did they know that the few times I did speak was much in my mind. At that time, I felt it was enough and didn't feel a need to explain that their values were not mine. All things happen when it is time.

Being amongst people with diverse backgrounds and cultures brought personal value systems to the forefront, or at least, I noticed it more. Growing up in Hawai'i, I knew people were different but wasn't aware that each had to undergo a personal process of determining what was of value. That determination seemed to be based on childhood experiences, and perhaps, even before. Perhaps those past experiences made us strong, weak, fearful, or whatever we felt and believed and determined the how and why of **choices** and personal agendas. It was a lesson, which instilled a consciousness and frequent reassessment of my values to delete old undesirables and acquire better ones. Those better ones helped me shed a number of my fears.

One fear I'm releasing to this day is writing badly. As an average writer in college, my freshman English instructor often said the subject choice was good, but he didn't quite understand what I wanted to say. I thought I did my best. Anyway, since then, I believed I was a poor writer and even disliked writing letters with the usual how-are-you and weather. Well, in grad school there were lots of required papers, and while I enjoyed doing research, that old fear was still with me, I dreaded putting information into writing and spent considerable time worrying how to write clearly so I wouldn't get the same feedback.

It was during a course, politics of planning, taught by Kem L., an urban planning instructor, I learned another lesson. I went to his office to retrieve my paper submitted earlier, and what a lucky break for me that he was in. As he handed me the paper, he said that the project I had researched was interesting, but there were parts, which left him wondering what I was trying to say. I wasn't offended because it was kind of an expected comment, one I had lived before. When I said to him, "I can't write well. I don't have a talent for writing", his immediate and abrupt response was, "Suen, writing is a skill, not a talent!" I was startled at first, but that statement brought instant revelation that I had been defeating myself before I had begun. My long time thought of being unable to do had become a self-fulfilling prophecy "Thots are things." It was a thought held which prolonged that inability, and it was time for another change.

It was a huge undertaking to affect that change, but I wanted to do it. It was a desire, a sincere desire, to become better than I had been. Why was it so important? I didn't and still don't really know, but that inner voice tells me there is much to do to reach oneness with the Almighty. To do that, I knew I had to make a conscious effort i.e. have conscious focus to remind and erase certain phrases from my mind—the controller of actions. Those phrases were, "I'm not capable, I can't do it, or I'll try." The words, "not" and "can't" were usually self-fulfilling prophecies while "try" left the door ajar for possible failure. If I tried and failed, it would be okay because I did put forth effort and would not lose face, an open door for redemption. I had to change those words to "can" and "will" for whatever I truly wanted to do. With God *all* things are possible, but I must *believe,* have *faith.*

I began to see that what I had "Thot" became a "thing." True, they're merely words, but words are an important part of our communication system and are vital to understand, accept, and peacefully live. Without doubt, words do have power for who can say they do not cause conflicts? They convey feelings and beliefs and cause actions.

How do I begin to become better? With questions of "How can I write better so others can understand what I'm trying to say, what kind of writing do I enjoy reading," and answers of "writing that's direct, to the point without a lot of words, so I won't forget the main point. So...do just that. You consider yourself direct, so get to the point with minimal verbiage and honor the importance of their time. Write as though you're conversing with them. Geez, maybe I'm wordy and confusing in conversations." Since many papers were required, practice was no problem. Gradually, I noticed an improvement, and with comments from the professors related to what I was saying on paper, I knew they understood. I also knew that becoming better was a dynamic and continuous process.

After about a year of school, I could see that health planning, or any planning was what I had been doing nearly all my life. Planning was especially important when I had to complete multiple tasks or responsibilities within a limited time frame. It was humorous to discover years later that all of us have been planning daily from our beginning for the now and the future. Planning should include contingency plans i.e. have another plan in case something happens and the first doesn't work out. I don't think many of us always plan for Murphy's Law, which states that if anything can go wrong, it will. Sometimes I do and sometimes I don't, depending on what it is, and if I'm able to think of something.

Without a doubt, I've been caught unaware at times and have done what planners label "incremental planning", and what I call a Band-aid approach, i.e. see one problem at a time, find a solution, forgetting that all things are part of a whole—interconnected.

Defining the problem was the first and most difficult step—the broad goal or policy statement, followed by more definitive objectives for solutions. Solutions decided, implementation or the actions followed, and of course, the whole process should be evaluated to determine if outcome was effective. If it wasn't, back to the drawing board.

Sounds simple, but it isn't. With so many people involved, especially in large projects, many different value systems interplay with personal, hidden, or open agendas. All is accompanied by time, that man- made clock, for a projected completion. A good example is our nation's Congress or our State legislature. I don't see their planning process differing from what we do daily, planning today for a tomorrow, the future.

When I stated to my program committee, a committee whose members were **chosen** by the student to help determine his/her graduation status, that everyone performed planning and that academia had merely demarcated and labeled parts of the process, they agreed. As a psychic once told me, planning was like throwing thoughts into shoeboxes to be retrieved some future day. That concept required lots of thought, but why not? We think of things we want to do in the future, some today, tomorrow, or years away, and it becomes, when needed, but more appropriately, when it is time. Sometimes those thoughts are forgotten until it happens, and we're awed or amazed by the results, attempting to understand the sequence of events.

Being a student again was unlike that of younger days. Before, school was just another hurdle to get over and not something I really felt like doing, but this time, there was a strong desire and determination. I was a sponge soaking in the pool of knowledge, not only about international events, culture, and health systems, but also about people with their thoughts, feelings, and actions—the political process.

Some call the political process a play composed of various actors singly or as groups, each with an agenda and a goal to achieve. I call it people interaction where interpersonal relationships and personal value systems determine the end result. As a child, I had heard the phrase, "people playing politics," but had never understood its meaning. I had heard it when someone was selected for or denied a choice position or contract, or when another was wined or dined for a favor. Even golf enters the play of creative and strategizing climates, and don't forget the Political Action Groups—PAC's.

It took formal education to show me that the political process is human interaction for a usually pre-determined end and is part of our daily lives. Others had learned it much sooner than I, but my time was then—"things happen when time." When it is time, that is, when I am ready to be taught, it will be, not before. It took a while for me to realize that a lesson had to be learned well before I was given another, i.e. I had to see with a clear vision, understand, and accept before another came. It seemed that when I learned quickly, progress accelerated and life became more enjoyable.

As a student, I had to work at chipping out the old glue and putting myself together with new. As months passed, I felt a change within, a change I called better because I could see better and more broadly. How did I know? By feedback from others who, when hearing my viewpoint, would say, "I never thought of it that way or that's good, that's different, let's think about it," etc. Feedback, another lesson from Bill G. and Jerry G., and reinforced by John H., a former boss, is a response to whatever, an expression of thoughts and feelings. I saw that placing my thoughts and ideas on the subject in the open was good, but I saw that expressing my feelings on the subject was more important. If I didn't, it would've been difficult to address whatever was being discussed because, internally, I'd be focused on how I felt, diverting my energy and focus. How then, could I give my best to the external topic? This is another lesson on how everything is inter-related, parts of the whole.

While studying, school seemed long, but when the end came, it suddenly seemed too short. Although graduation was a culmination of a longtime desire, I didn't feel ready to face the world in a new field. I asked myself, "Now what? I have a Master of Public Health—so what? What can I really do...where do I go...where do I begin?" The school didn't have a placement service so graduates were on their own. Some positions were found via the grapevine. My focus had been primarily on entering, keeping up, and graduating, not on finding a job, my shortsightedness, but I was optimistic and believed something would come along—call it faith.

I could have moved back to the mainland where opportunities were plentiful, but I didn't want that, so an extra effort in job hunting was required. Returning to the laboratory field wasn't a considered option because it would have defeated my purpose of returning to school. I did, however, decide to give myself respite before serious job hunting.

X

MOM'S PASSING

$\mathcal{M}$om died five months before I graduated, and although I missed her then, I felt her absence more after graduation. Between school, children, and property management, I was too busy to allow myself to really feel her absence, but I still felt a void, the same emptiness I had when Bud died. I recalled what a niece had said to me when Mom died, "I bet you're relieved." I was surprised and momentarily speechless by her statement because it inferred a presumption that I was glad she had died. I thought about her words for a moment, asking myself if I did feel relief. I did feel some release from seeing to another's needs, but this was my mother whom I loved very much and who always showed her love even during my college years—unconditional love. I looked at my niece and slowly nodded in response, knowing full well that I felt more sadness and emptiness than relief, but I knew she wouldn't understand if I expressed it. How could she when I saw her world not yet expanded. Her statement told me that she was expressing how she would feel if or when she had to care for her parents on a long-term basis. It was another episode, which taught me how spoken words revealed the person.

With Mom gone, I knew it would take a while to adjust. My daily routine with her was rising early to make breakfast and feed her. After breakfast, she had a bath, change of clothing, and fresh bedding. Every morning, I would rise early and start for her room, only to remember that she was gone. She had been so much a part of our lives that the children and I missed seeing and talking with her. She was my mother, good- natured and pleasant, who never scolded me when I sassed her, and who showed me she cared.

When I went on a date or out with friends, she'd lie awake in bed until I returned, emerge from the bedroom, and say to me in Korean, "You're home," and when I answered yes, would go to bed. It was a ritual I didn't like because I felt I was grownup, but became so accustomed to it that, on rare occasions if she didn't greet me when I returned, I'd open my parents' bedroom door and peek in. I had to make sure *she* was in bed. She usually awakened to acknowledge my presence, but occasionally, did not. Those times I closed the door quietly and went to bed. I grumbled at her for being such a worrywart, but much later after I had left home, I realized and understood it was her way of saying she loved me.

I didn't know the huge responsibility parents had until I had to care for my own family. Even then, I thought it was easy until challenged by their teen years when lots of problems surfaced. By then, nothing I said or did to made any difference in their behavior. They had become members of that all-too-smart-know-it-all club, with back talk loud or whispered, bored or expressionless faces, eyes rolling up and slouched postures, answering before I completed a sentence. I had read and heard of other parents' experiences, but still wasn't prepared for mine. Funny how only in retrospect I saw the awesome responsibility of caring for children, but then, retrospective understanding and acceptance was usually the norm, coming all too slowly. Nonetheless, the important lesson learned was I could not control anyone but myself. It turned out to be a very long lesson of many years.

Caring for Mom was payback for what my parents did for me. It was only after I had my own family, I appreciated my parents more, who they were and what they did. Oh sure, all wasn't rosy, but I considered them pioneers like those from other countries. They took the risk of leaving their country, Korea, bonded themselves to plantation work in a strange land filled with strange peoples, languages, and customs. As strangers in a new land, they kept to their ethnic group, as others did with theirs, keeping language, beliefs, and customs intact and helping each other as needed. That didn't mean that ethnic lines weren't crossed when there was need.

One doctor and a very small hospital provided plantation health care, but most families depended on home remedies shared amongst the peoples. It was the time of old-time remedies which many families adhere to today and which the National Institute of Health calls "alternative medicine"—a contemporary label, bringing its importance to the forefront and the reasons why so many of us still use it—*it works.*

Before the time of routine tetanus shots, a deep cut on my foot or nail injury meant Dad would prepare a hot bucket of water with Epsom salt and make me soak my foot until the wound was clean. By then the water had cooled, and he would apply topical antiseptic and dress it. A doctor, shot, or hospital wasn't part of our lives until much later.

Hospitals were for the seriously ill who usually died there.

Knowing Mom's intense dislike for hospitals after a bad experience of being tied to her bed, I decided she should spend her last moments at home. This was during the time when dying with dignity was being publicly discussed as the right of every individual. Her bad experience happened after a stroke while I lived on the mainland. When I returned home, my sister told me what had happened. She had attempted to use the bathroom when she fell before reaching it and alarmed the nurses who decided to tie her wrists to the bed to keep her from further harm. Because none spoke or understood Korean, they were unable to help her. By the time my sister visited her, she was distraught and screaming. From that time Dad made certain she was cared for at home and arranged for Auntie, Mom's youngest sister-in-law, to come from Korea and care for her. It was Mom's intense dislike for the hospital and the home arrangement Dad had in place, which influenced my decision to keep her at home until she died. I had decided for her with the family knowing, but I felt she would have agreed.

I remember the night she departed. She was weaker and not very responsive but still managed to squeeze my hand. When the family came to see her, one sister suggested I send her to the hospital. She was concerned that it would be too difficult for me to have Mom die at home. In a way, she was right about it being difficult because I wasn't looking forward to it, but I was determined to follow my belief that Mom would have decided the same if she could, and she had the right to die in a surrounding she loved. I refused, telling her that I would be all right, but I wasn't absolutely certain I would be. After everyone left, I went into Mom's room and held her hand. As she held my hand tightly, I softly told her in pidgin Korean that it was okay to go to God. I sat with her for a while then released her hand to join my son in the living room. We sat quietly, eyes downcast, each in thought, when suddenly it seemed too quiet. We looked at each other, jumped up, and ran into her room. She was gone, left us, and as I touched her, I felt an overwhelming sadness at her departure. It was a time to again ask why be born only to die? Is our purpose on Earth only to be born and die or is Earth our hell to which we repeatedly return and correct our errors or complete unfinished business? What is heaven and can we create heaven on Earth?

I believe Earth is our hell, if that's what I want to call it, but I also believe we can create heaven, that beautiful place to live in on Earth. I think we create our own hell, through our **choices** and actions, but when we **choose** to become better and in becoming better help others to do the same, we create our heaven, not alone, but together.

As I stood at Mom's bedside, looking at her peaceful face, I told myself call the family and the doctor. I called my sister first and she took care of notifying everyone including Mom's attending physician. Feeling weary I was grateful for her offer, and anyway, I didn't like being the bearer of bad news. The doctor came quickly enough, and after examining her, told me the cause of death was congestive heart failure. I thought for a moment and asked him why not put cause of death, as it was her time. In his usual serious, poker-faced manner, he informed me it wasn't an appropriate cause. Sometimes so-called appropriateness isn't the truth.

Mom was in her eighties and had enjoyed her life. She always spoke of living a long time until one day, not long before her death, she said it was time to die. I was stunned by her statement, and yet, I knew by the way she said it, she felt it was time to depart. It was also her lack of appetite and decreasing enthusiasm and strength that told me she would soon leave us. She just seemed tired of continuing. I hope, by the time I die, I can have for cause of death, **It's My Choice!** because it will be.

XI

SEARCHING FOR AND BUYING A HOME

*W*ith Mom gone, it was time to seriously look for work and a place to live, but since her property would be in probate for about a year, according to the attorney, I didn't feel hurried. My sense of rootlessness prevailed while living with Mom for two years, but now that what I had returned to do was finished, it was time to move on and find out what more I had to live.

At first, I wanted to buy Mom's property and had mentioned it to my sister who was one of Dad's executors. The house was fifty years old and needed a lot of work, but it was where I grew up with good memories. I felt the children and I could fix it up nicely although I was a little concerned that I may not have enough funds to do all of it. Anyway, those ambitious thoughts weren't meant to be. My sister wanted to help me by setting the sale price below appraisal value, and my eldest brother, the other executor, agreed to go along, but the others wanted to sell it for the best market price and what should be "fair" to all. We met at our eldest brother's home to determine what everyone wanted to do, and as I listened to each of them, my gut feeling said look for another home, your very own, and do it without help from the family, on your own. It told me that this had been the home of my youth, but it was time for another family to live in it with enjoyment. In order to stand on my own two feet, I had to purchase a house alone. I was not to receive help with emotional strings attached. If they had sold me our parents' home below appraisal value, I would be beholden to all forever, disabling my desire to do it on my own. I wasn't absolutely certain I would succeed, but I had to make an earnest attempt to take the risk. That reason held fast when I wanted cash out when the property was sold instead of receiving double digit interest on an agreement of sale. My sister tried several times to persuade me to join them because I'd benefit financially, and though it was a nice thought, it meant postponing looking for a home at least another year. I felt an urgency to find out if I could stand on my own two feet—that symbolic representation of life's foundation, and the time had come.

I didn't fault those who wanted to maximize their share. After all, charity does begin at home, and it was an opportunity to help themselves and their families. Besides, I had heard stories of financial conflicts within families and among siblings in settling parents' estates, a most unpleasant situation, creating division, lasting their lifetime. I had to be free of ties and begin without conflict and regret, or I would encounter future stumbling blocks. So, I embarked on another important lesson to stand on my own two feet, to know who I am and what I had in me.

When Mom's probate was finally over, it was time to look for a place to live. Fortunately for me, the real estate market was down, allowing time to check various areas. I didn't enlist the help of a realtor because I felt it would involve dealing with pressure from a sales pitch. I only knew that when I found a place, somehow, I would know it was right for me.

In looking for a home, I first had to think of what was most importance i.e. prioritized criteria, a process many of us go through for important decisions. There were three, which mattered most: price, distance to and from work, and traffic. Price because I would be spending my future income for thirty years with no guarantee of continuous employment even though I was optimistic of remaining gainfully employed. With my dislike for driving, distance and heavy traffic weren't an acceptable combination. They didn't mix well, especially after listening to people living in the newer areas away from town. They spoke of having to leave one to two hours before work time and spend almost as long going home. From that I developed a strong conviction that distance was a definite disadvantage, and if I wanted to live within my means, I had to consider all costs, including travel. With home prices more attractive further from town, it wasn't easy to decide to stick close to town especially after seeing the lovely new homes. I suppose my dislike for driving long distances, which, on this island, is like twenty or more miles, comes from driving long distances on the mainland, spending a short time at the destinations, and retracing those same distances. Call it insular mentality from growing up on an island.

It seemed like a long time before I decided, but this was a major, major decision. My final **choice** was to remain in the same area where I grew up. It's close to schools, church, shopping centers and work, isn't too damp, dry, or hot as some other areas, and has a nice valley breeze. It is a special place with frequent rainbows, giving a special feeling. It's not where the wealthy and upper middle class live but is my kind of community with ordinary working and retired people of all ages and ethnicity, living in modest homes. With that decision made, it was time to find a home.

Looking for a home meant going through the classified section in the daily paper several times a week, and it wasn't too long before I found one. It may sound odd, but I can't recall doubting that I would find one in the area I wanted. I called the number listed and spoke with the owner, whose voice I recognized as one I had spoken with two months before when I first began house hunting. At that time, his selling price was ten thousand dollars more, a price beyond my reach, but now, the price was considerably less because he no longer used a realtor. He said the price was reasonable, but to me, Hawai'i home prices have never been reasonable.

Homes have always been overpriced and wages haven't kept up with prices. Why should they? We love our Island State and don't want to live anywhere else, and so, have **chosen** to become a captive employee and consumer population. It's not unusual to be jerked around by high prices for basic human needs and extras, making sales a popular means of getting customers into the stores. To benefit the best from a sale, people go early, sometimes before the doors open. Many don't want to live anywhere else, so are willing to work for lower wages and pay the high cost of living. I wouldn't doubt if this State has the highest number of working married couples and persons with two or more jobs.

With in-migration and an influx of investors, demand for homes exceeded supply, escalating home prices to what seemed like a point of no return. It wasn't uncommon to see homes listing for a million or more. If that trend continues, though it can be slower during a lackluster economy, Hawai'i will become a paradise for the wealthy.

As I listened to the owner's description of the house with the capability of fixing the downstairs as a rental and the ample land in the back to build another house, all I could think of was how much I should commit for a down payment. His other selling points didn't interest me simply because my priority was to find a home for the four of us. As I wondered if I could qualify for a home loan, he offered a five-year agreement of sale. I was surprised that he had picked up on my thoughts but was glad because it was an opportunity to learn more of its workings.

It didn't take long to learn its process. Such an arrangement can be from one to however many years the seller was willing to go. At that time, the usual period was three to five years with buyer paying the owner monthly interest until the end of the agreed upon time when a balloon payment was due. This allowed the buyer time to seek commercial financing for the balloon payment. I had heard that buyers who didn't have or didn't want to pay the required down payment by a bank often used it. It allowed time to save and qualify for a commercial loan, while investors used it to leverage their buy and sell prior to due date, usually at a profit. With that financing decision made, we set a day and time to meet at the house.

When that day arrived, I found myself driving up a dead-end street. Not bad, I thought, few homes, and it looked like a quiet neighborhood. He said it was the last house on the street. It was a house sitting on the lower slope of a mountain. The home faced East, which appealed to me because facing the sun at the beginning of the day represents light along my path. I parked and met the owner who was already there. As I walked up the many steps, I scanned the yard, if I could call it that. It was more like a huge field of haole koa and rich green growth more than four feet tall with seeded tassels towering over me. I gave a big sigh because it meant that I'd never run out of something to do, but that wasn't so important then.

The house was more important, that is, how I felt about it. I was determined to purchase a home intuitively, a strange **choice**, but my **choice**, nonetheless. As I slowly made my way through, I thought the rooms were small, including the baths and kitchen, but the view nice and expansive. However, the most important thing was the increasing sense of calm and the strong drawing I had, telling me that I had come home.

It was a house built by a Japanese man in his sixties who had learned his trade in Japan. According to a neighbor, he had built the house alone with only occasional help to hoist the heavy beams. It was a marvel to picture one man applying his skills and talents to building a house just as it's a marvel to see how multi-storied structures come to fruition even though am not fond of them.

I can't say that many tall buildings have extraordinary architecture, but their height gives them a unique appearance. Building upward is considered practical use of limited space, but it compacts people, increases traffic, challenges patience, flares tempers and creates pollution and other problems. Still, I'm amazed at the result of human creativity "Thots are things". It's a "Thot" created today that becomes a "thing" tomorrow just as my "thot" for a home became a "thing" when I found one.

Satisfied with my decision, I asked the owner when would be a good time to open the house again so I could bring my sister and brother-in-law. On the set day, I pointed to the house as we drove up the street.

My sister was silent for a moment then emphatically said, "I don't like it!" My immediate and equally emphatic reply was, "*I* like it", with emphasis on I. She said the large boulders further up the mountain might roll down, crashing into the house. Her fear stemmed from a boulder crashing into a Manoa Valley couple's home, crushing them. I told her that I didn't have the feeling it would happen with this property, but I knew she wasn't convinced. I understood and appreciated her concern for me, but I felt it was to be my home, not hers. If boulders came crashing down, it would be *my* **chosen** risk not anyone else's and therefore, my **chosen** time to depart. When it is time, it will happen.

As a side note, a boulder did come crashing down one early morning after a few days of heavy rains. It demolished the doghouse twenty feet from the back of the house. Not too many days before the rains, I had moved the dog to the back lanai because a neighbor had complained of his barking, a natural happening when her cat sat on the rock formation out of his reach. She wasn't the best of neighbors, but her complaint saved my dog. I suppose I should have thanked her.

When my sister and her husband finished walking through the house, the four of us stood by the front door. The owner turned to my brother-in-law, reiterating his reasonable sale price, to begin what I saw as negotiation. Without hesitation, my brother-in-law countered with five thousand dollars less. I was surprised and somewhat irritated when he responded because my offer would have been a reduction twice that. I hadn't asked or indicated that I wanted him to dicker price for me. After all, it was my money, and he should have consulted with me first. True, it was my first solo humungous purchase, but I had brought them for a second opinion, primarily because of my sister's innate ability to spot good property. It was only after, I realized the importance of communicating my purpose for asking them, but the deed was done and the offer set—another lesson in communication.

I failed to speak up when the owner turned to my brother-in-law to discuss price probably due to fear, inexperience, and uncertainty of the process and outcome. The price was disappointing even knowing that my brother-in-law, with a realtor's license though not actively selling, was only trying to help, a thought I did appreciate.

Being ignored, though not maliciously, was just another repeat of how many traditional and even contemporary men usually treat women— as though ignorant and incapable to do what is still known as "man's work or business." Women can learn and do as well as men and sometimes better, just as men can learn and do "woman's work" as well or better. Physiologically, all have male and female hormones, complements to each other, so "where's the beef?" If we can remember we're but parts of the whole, of each other, of our Earth, we'll see our connective role to maintain balance not differences, which can cause chaos and problems.

The owner was anxious to set a day to close the deal, but I told him I wanted a few more days to think it over. Those few days were filled with mixed emotions as I vacillated between uncertainty and confidence. I wanted to purchase it but panicked when I thought of the tremendous financial responsibility and wondered if I could manage payments for thirty years. What'll happen if I'm ill unable to work, who'll make the payments? I'd never ask or rely on the children; they have struggles of their own. On the other hand, I had fleeting moments of confidence that I had already decided, that all things would fall into place and go well, and that I needn't worry. As the time drew near, I believed that my first **choice** would stand because it followed my gut feeling. I knew that it would keep me from total financial independence for a long time, but someday I would reach that personal goal.

Having decided, I called the owner who arranged for me to meet with his accountant to sign the agreement of sale papers. The accountant wanted me to meet him in a restaurant, a strange place to sign such important papers, but I felt it was okay. He was a mature soft- spoken man who explained the terms and payment arrangement and made certain I understood them before handing me the pen to sign. The terms were to pay interest only for the first year after which time I could pay on principal too.

While signing the papers, that human frailty, fear, surfaced again to doubt my decision. "What am I doing signing my life away to be chained forever to a material good." It was the biggest step I had taken alone, and it felt scary, lonely. It was one of the rare times I wished I had someone to lean on, if only for a moment. Transaction completed, he gave me the agreement papers, which I carefully folded and placed in my purse. We shook hands, and I thanked him for explaining everything.

Driving back to Mom's house, I didn't feel euphoria or happiness only a great sense of relief and release. The relief was from **choosing** where I would settle, probably my last, and the release was from the sense of rootlessness, of not belonging anywhere since we had left Arizona. I was home to stay.

It was about a year after we had moved into our new home that I decided to sell the townhouse in Phoenix. The year's wait was purposeful. I had to be certain I could handle the monthly payments for the new house before selling the townhouse, but more importantly, that moving to Hawai'i was right. During that year, there seemed to be more problems with the townhouse, telling me it was time to sell. It was difficult being an absentee landlord and finding a rental manager. I wasn't satisfied with the current agent, a realtor, who often told me, whenever he called with a problem, that units sold quickly. My mistake was to think aloud that perhaps I should sell when he called about replacing the air conditioner compressor. He quickly picked up on it and offered his services. I told him I wasn't ready, but when he called with other problems, he'd ask if I had decided to sell. After the third time, I wearied of his reminders and pressure and spit out a volley of words. I said that I wasn't stupid and could see through his scheme with his commission as primary. As he stammered out his denial, I reminded him that during the last few calls he always told me how good the market was and that he'd be glad to help me. I surprised myself by saying so much, and yes, I could have been gentler, but my emotional human side felt it was time to speak assertively or was it aggressively? Anyway, I felt better after that release and realized that suppressing what I wanted to say, whenever he called, made me tense and irritable. I knew that I had to become more responsible for my emotions i.e. take charge of myself more. Getting irritable or angry at what others said or did wasn't helping me progress. It only made me react rather than confronting what I had in me. I could have, frankly and calmly, told him the same thing without anger, transcending that emotion.

I needed to stop internalizing so much and speak my mind especially when I have strong feelings, providing it's appropriate, calm, honest, and timely. It was a risky **choice** for me who didn't say much except when with family and required many practices before I began to feel comfortably unembarrassed. Practicing continues to this day. Living is full of practice, isn't it?

As I settled into our new home, I found that it was not only a really big financial responsibility, but also a physically demanding one.

Clearing the property of its tall weeds and haole koa trees was a major project and having to use a sickle and medium-sized pick as regular tools didn't qualify me as a lady gardener. There was no room for daintiness. Relatives and my son's friends helped but keeping up is a year-round project, especially after rain. One thing was and still is certain, procrastination never worked with yard tasks because the weeds, vines, and brush only grew bigger and tougher, requiring more time and energy to dig them up. The natural slope of the mountain not only sent heavy rainwater cascading down at a high rate of speed, it also let soil and unwanted seeds wash down. It took several years and numerous attempts before I had some visual sense of a cared for yard. In the beginning, I had a rough mental plan of where I wanted trees and small plants, but with the rocky terrain above and below ground level, that went by the wayside.

Instead, there were frequent lessons in flexibility, adjustment, and contingency plans when my pick hit rock. I finally gave in to Mother Earth and planted wherever there was sufficient depth for the plant or tree, and though I never knew if it would survive, I was always hopeful. If it didn't, I changed the plant or location. One thing I know for certain is that Mother Earth does rule this yard. Today, it's a potpourri of plants and trees stuck wherever my pick didn't hit rock along with the weeds which still insist on keeping me company with the ants, centipedes, roaches, and various other insects, in this subtropical haven. Oddly enough, it does present a pleasant picture even to family and friends.

There's still much more to do, but it'll have to wait until my "golden years" when I hope to have more time with enough physical ability.

XII

JOB HUNTING

$\mathscr{I}$n recalling how I found a job, I thought it was luck, but later realized it was another meant to be—an episode that affirmed things happen when time. A private, non-profit planning agency had received Federal funding to organize citizen participation in the State. Oahu had seventy-five percent of the population and with a recently signed public law for health planning to include grassroots involvement, the agency believed that the island should have more than the one already existing and recognized by the State, Windward Oahu. The agency staff recognized three additional areas that also deserved official recognition, Waianae, West Oahu, and East Honolulu where I lived. When the agency held their first public meeting in my area, I attended.

The meeting began with the agency's presentation emphasizing the importance of organizing health planning councils for grassroots participation. After the presentation, we broke into small groups facilitated by agency staff. During our discussion, I spoke of a past personal need for information of available community resources to assist family caretakers of the elderly. I said I could have used respite services, but didn't know if any were available, so used the only resource I knew of—the classified ad and asked if others had similar needs.

Listening in our group was John H., Director of the agency's health planning program, and who, I feel, was responsible for my being offered a job. It was one of the staff planners who asked if I would be interested in working for the agency. The offer, totally unexpected, was welcomed as a chance to see if health planning really was for me. She told me that the position was temporary long as Federal funds held out. The salary was less than what the State paid their planners, but I didn't care. I was grateful for the chance to become involved in health planning and was prepared to use what I had learned though still unsure as to how I'd use it. I wondered if health planning would be my niche, so the only way to find out was to do it.

My boss was Helen M., a thoughtful, articulate woman who believed in grassroots involvement in planning. Initially, she assigned me to do legislative research for the agency, which involved checking the agency's box at the legislature for copies of bills and resolutions generated by the State House and Senate. My job was to read and analyze them for health and social issues that the community council of the agency would want to address. The Council members were leaders or representatives of various community and government organizations in the State, and of labor, health, and social agencies. Being so different from clinical lab work, I was anxious in the beginning because of wanting to do my best but eventually felt comfortable with the task. After the State legislature had ended for the year, she introduced me to the tasks of a health planner as she organized the Waianae Coast Subarea Health Planning Council.

The Waianae Coast is a unique non-contiguous part of O'ahu, encompassing Nanakuli, Maile, Waianae, and Makaha. Some time ago, it had been identified as a socially and economically depressed area by the State and Federal governments and had received funds through the Model Cities, Community Action, Progressive Neighborhood, and Maternal and Child Health Programs. It also had been designated a judicial district, so it seemed natural to consider the whole area as a subarea for health planning. To organize, we contacted various community organizations along the coast to attend an organizational meeting, providing staff support for the first and subsequent meetings. Staff support involved researching State and Federal legislation, Federal rules and regulations and laws, preparing public testimony for council members, preparing members to present testimonies, coordinating meetings, preparing agendas, and numerous other tasks.

Working with members of the Council was an experience. The members, veterans in the State's political process, knew what they wanted and didn't hesitate to make it known. They were an assertive and "Akamai" (Hawaiian for smart) group who knew what grassroots organization and participation were about. I still smile when I think of how much I've learned from them. They showed me that involvement and information were necessary for action to "affect change." They believed in a direct, firm, yet mannerly approach, keeping abreast of changes. They understood human nature and its propensity to change openly or behind closed doors. The most important lesson for me was their **choice** to control their own lives and to deter those who wanted to **choose** for them. They knew their community's information base and were capable in planning for themselves. They believed in the feedback system that told anyone like it was and articulated their thoughts and feelings well. Even today I can't help but smile when I read or hear of any Waianae group speaking against changes planned by those who do not live there.

It was another lesson from Drs. Jerry G. And Bill G. that to "affect change", working through the system, however long, would usually be the path of least resistance.

To this day, my six months at the agency was the best position I have had. It was intense with long hours, but the fruits of labor and lessons learned were worth every day spent there. Staff interaction was such that we worked as a team helping each other in coordinating and attending meetings, critiquing writings, and generally being supportive of each other. Management didn't hover about us or look over our shoulders, and if something needed correcting, it wasn't a big thing for we knew it had to be done. I didn't feel offended when corrected for I knew that all experiences were lessons for me and was grateful for the time they took to teach me. The climate was open, trusting, and conducive for frank expressions without fear of oppression or ridicule. We listened and were listened to i.e. to the explicit and implicit messages. As I listened and learned, I better understood and accepted other's perspectives. I learned to develop and strengthen flexibility, one of the key ingredients in making change possible.

Learning about the legislative process was also an invaluable experience as I saw our State legislators striving to do what was best for the State, their community and themselves, all of which results didn't always coincide. They, too, had to **choose**. This process was further affirmation of my perception that personal value systems *do* have impact on decisions, even major ones. That's scary. It taught me that unless I **choose** to become informed, others will **choose** for me and to allow that is also my **choice**.

The dynamics of living bring changes, which we may want to postpone. In a way, I wanted to do just that when it was time to leave the agency, but I knew that it was time to think of what I was to do next. It was time to ask myself if health planning was right for me, did I have what it takes, and if I wanted to do it the rest of my life. In self-assessing, I didn't feel I had been as effective as I would have liked and seriously doubted my capabilities. It was time to find out, so I asked my supervisor. This came about because I had applied for and had been selected for a clinical laboratory technologist position. The temporary position was coming to an end, and I needed a permanent job to pay for living expenses. To my surprise, my request made her very uncomfortable. I understood her hesitation because it wasn't the kind of feedback in which she wanted involvement for whatever reason. She waited until another day before slowly and tactfully telling me that I should allow more time in planning before deciding to return to lab. I felt that six months were long enough to get some sense of how anyone was doing and had hoped for a more direct answer. I also wondered how she defined long one year, two. No matter, she told me what I already knew but didn't want to accept— formal health planning wasn't for me. It's my feeling that, if she had perceived me as competent, she probably wouldn't have hesitated, so it was time to move on. I enjoyed working with everyone and was somewhat sad in leaving, but my inner told me I had more learning to do. I wasn't certain as to what next, and although I knew it wouldn't be in health planning, it would be somewhere requiring planning, an integral part of our lives.

While at the agency, family life still had its ups and downs. One episode that comes to mind is when my son was injured in a motorcycle accident near Sandy Beach, a favorite of body surfers. The day before his accident, I was angry with him, for what, I can't recall. I told him that if he didn't want to abide by my rules, he could leave. I had a habit of telling the children they could leave if they felt too grownup to follow my house rules. Angry, he hopped on his motorcycle, a dangerous vehicle in my opinion, and drove away. He didn't return that night, and I became concerned, hoping that he was staying with his friend.

The next day, work at the planning agency was unusually slow, a first time for us, so I left early to reach home just before three in the afternoon. I was catching up on household tasks when my older daughter told me someone, a stranger, was calling to ask how my son was. That query and her worried look told me something had happened. I dropped everything and hurried to the phone, listening to the caller asking how my son was doing. Instead of answering, I asked him what he meant and he replied, "Oh wow, you don't know? The police didn't tell you?" I said, "No, they didn't. What happened?" He told me that my son, while riding his motorcycle, hit the rear fender of his car, flew through the air, and landed on the ground. He had waited until the ambulance arrived to take my son to Tripler, the military hospital, and was calling to find out if he was okay. He thought the police had contacted me and apologized for being the first to give me bad news. As I listened to this stranger caring enough to inquire about my son, it told me that there still are people out there who cared—a personal reminder to tenaciously embrace faith and hope for there *is* light. Sometimes we need to look harder and longer for it.

The police never notified me, and I didn't know if that was part of their service, but thanks to the stranger, I knew where my son was. Perhaps the police thought the hospital would notify the family, but the hospital didn't either. It was scary when I thought of how I may not have found out at all, but in this situation, there was one person who followed through when official channels failed. Things happen for a reason and when it is time. After thanking the caller, I immediately called the hospital and was told he was in surgery. He had a compound fracture of his arm and a fractured pelvis, but his condition was good. I thanked God that he had the benefit of youthful health and believed he would mend quickly.

When I visited him in the hospital, I saw he was still angry with me, retaliating with silence, but I think he was inwardly glad I was there. His doctor had left for the day so I asked him what was done. He said the doctor had inserted a metal rod through the two separated bones to be removed at a later time. He was also told that a bone chip, floating above the arm bone, might not move down to fuse. I couldn't accept the thought of it not fusing and visualized it adhering to and fusing strongly to the bone. I also told my son to use his own inner energy and focus his thoughts on all his bones mending well and strongly. He said he already was doing just that. I don't know how long his arm took to heal, but heal it did, with all parts together.

For me, visualization is part of "Thots are things", which I use often to maintain good health not only for family and myself, but also for others whom I see as not well. I believe that for "Thot" to become a "thing", belief is necessary. To desire isn't enough, but to believe that it will be is the key. It is *faith*. I believe that we can heal ourselves by wanting and believing we can, an integral part of loving ourselves. Belief is the confidence of knowing, an inner knowing, that we can do whatever if we so **choose**. Desire is the beginning of **choice** and belief is the substance, which carries it through. Together, they gel into action, resulting in progress, a growing within, to cope with all matters in living. It is part of the healing process we go through for our mind, body, and spirit. A healing brings balance to each of us, to those around us, and to the world we live in—our Mother Earth.

XIII

JOB HUNTING AGAIN

After two weeks of relaxing, it was time to do some serious job hunting. The first place I applied to was the State's largest health insurance plan. I didn't know how or where I could fit into the organization, but felt I had nothing and a no would be the worst of that effort. I called the personnel office and was encouraged when the personnel tech said I could qualify for their management trainee program. I hurried down and waited until the personnel tech reviewed my application. Having completed her review and interview, she explained their management trainee program and asked if I was interested. I said yes, and she further explained that I had to take a couple tests, a surprising first and different from applying at a clinical laboratory. Besides needing a job, this new process piqued my curiosity, so I agreed to the test taking. I must have done okay because after a while I was ushered into the personnel director's office for another interview.

He was a pleasant, kindly, corpulent gentleman, who, after asking a series of questions, concluded the interview with a statement that I would be given an appointment for another interview with the two senior vice- presidents. He warned me that a couple applicants had been intimidated by their size, both being six feet tall, and their barrage of questions angered one applicant. He shared that information to eliminate the element of surprise and I thanked him.

When the day came for that interview, I went in anticipating a grueling bout and was prepared to walk out if necessary, but instead of a third degree, I was surprised by their straightforward approach.

Following questions regarding my experience, there was a pause as they discussed between themselves, the two areas that needed additional staffing then concluded the interview saying that I would be notified of a decision within a week following two more interviews. Well, instead of two, I had one more interview and was informed that I would hear from them soon. Whew! That long process was finally over.

I had considered applying to the hospitals as other graduates because that seemed the most prominent option when I returned to school, but that thought didn't excite me. Most of my prior work experience, though technical in nature, had been in hospitals, and while the administrative aspect would be new to me, the overall setting was not. I definitely wanted to explore something different.

Working for a third-party payer, as health insurance plans are called, would be different, and I'd still be in the health field where I wanted to remain. The more I thought of the health plan position, the more I felt it would be a better position for me. While living in Phoenix, I had wondered how health plans were administered, and had thought that perhaps one day I would work for one "Thots" are "things". It seemed I was completing a full circle in the health field by first working with health care providers in hospitals and clinics, consumers in the community for health planning, and now third-party payers. Actually we, the consumers, are the payers, through private premiums and government taxes. Of course, medical supply is the only area I haven't experienced, but it seemed I was meant to experience the three areas to expand my perception and perspective.

Two weeks after my last interview at the health plan association, a former colleague at the health planning agency where I had worked called to ask if I would be interested in doing a short-term program evaluation. Definitely, I said if the health plan didn't hire me and told her that I'd find out and let her know. I queried the personnel office and explained that I had another job offer and wondered if a decision to hire had been made. The secretary said she would find out and let me know soon as possible. They called the next day to tell me that I was to begin in their management trainee program of three months. I immediately called my friend and declined her offer. If her offer had been a permanent position, I would have been inclined to accept because it would have been challenging in terms of analysis and recommendation, abilities I wanted to develop further. I had no clue that the position I had accepted would give me just that. It was another thing which became "Thots are things".

The management trainee program was three months of fairly intensive classroom and on the job training in claims review and processing, fiscal management which included rate setting, professional relations with health care providers, and other areas that turned the wheels of plan management. The overall concept and theme for the health association was cost containment, the two elusive words and process our government and business still strive to realize.

My salary also carried the cost containment theme, but employee benefits and working climate were quite good with everyone so friendly and helpful. I wondered how such a large group of compatible individuals came together. Was the interview and selection process designed in such a way that the ability to work together was priority? Perhaps. Anyway, having a permanent position was a godsend and a must because, with Mom's probate closing, it meant I had to look for a home very soon.

After training, I was assigned first as staff assistant, becoming supervisor later, to a unit involved in research and analysis and identifying utilization trends of health care services. While we used a number of sources, the primary source of information was claims submitted for services rendered. Since claims information was computerized, it provided a large information base from which further in-depth studies were possible. It was after I had been there a while, working with and seeing the multiple ways information could be used, I realized its power. I thought of the Internal Revenue Service with its tremendous information base and legal clout and its knowledge of how much taxpayers earned, spent, saved, or invested, and even where they saved or invested. With its legal power, it seemed almost futile to contest its penalties or actions, but I also knew that it had the human factor for making errors. I wondered why our world seemed so intent in information gathering and where was the stop point for it. Computers made work more efficient and faster, but I am not sure faster is always better especially when data entry is erroneous.

Everyone's in the act of information gathering and processing. Banks and merchants accumulate it through their charge cards. They know what you spend money on and market their goods accordingly. Applying for cards opens the door to develop people's profiles—where we live and how we live with desires and habits known through savings, withdrawals, and purchases. What assurance do I have that my privacy has not or would not be invaded? Absolutely none! Today, there's still the trend for financial institutions to share teller machines, while catalog purchases open the door for name selling to other commercial entities, making me a victim of daily junk mail. If I don't want my name given to others, according to the fine print which can be easily missed, a written statement to that effect is required. Why should I bear the burden of taking the time and expense of saying no? I'd prefer it to be a given that no names be traded or sold unless I expressly check a yes box.

With the economic changes in Europe: no trade barriers, open door travel from one country to another, and still to come, a unified money system, will there also be one card for all transactions? How will all these changes affect the rest of the world? Will the whole world join the one card concept? That means information will travel faster than us humans. My inner tells me we may as well drop the word "privacy" from our vocabulary. If we all join that one card club, all information will be fed into the computer and filed, and we become numbers with all information centralized. I wonder if that wouldn't fulfill the Bible's Revelations. A mere flick of the wrist and fingers could access anyone's value system with past, present, and probable future activities determined—a total profile. I shudder at the thought that a stranger could know who I am, my interest, and my comings or goings. What's my other option? Become independent. Owe no one and barter or purchase with cash. I can **choose** to become independent, ruler of my world not someone else's. It's easy to say, but difficult to do, and yet, I see it as an ongoing challenge that's possible to fulfill, an independence, which doesn't negate inter-connectedness. With God, *all* things are possible.

XIV

TENDING TO HEALTH

*N*ow that I was settled, rooted in one place, thoughts turned to self. I had gained more weight than was good for me, and it was time to do something. I believed in good health, but obviously I didn't practice it. I could be disciplined in other areas, but when it came to food, I had none.

It wasn't any help when others brought me chocolates with nuts, my favorite, and of course, I didn't ration them for multiple days. I definitely wanted to lose and feel healthy besides looking presentable, but my hearty appetite and love for sweets overshadowed that desire. Many previous attempts failed, and it seemed I was permanently locked into a losing battle of the bulge until my brother asked about my blood pressure. He suggested I jog as he did, which was then the newest sport craze. I thought well, maybe.

I had seen many people jogging and running who looked trim and healthy, and though I wanted to look that good too, I wasn't sure that was for me. I visualized myself jogging but could only see profuse sweating, feet heavily pounding the ground as I huffed and puffed with great effort. Nah, that wasn't for me. Swimming was better but getting wet more than several times a week wasn't appealing either, so I put exercising on hold a little while longer. Reason was caring for Mom, but to be honest I wasn't ready—it wasn't time.

It was only after I had begun working at the health plan, I decided, after some persuasion and encouragement from co-workers, to join its newly formed jogging group. A few avid marathoners were forming a group of first-time joggers, and since I didn't have an excuse, it was time to begin. We met after work several times a week and began slow jogging around Ala Moana Park's Magic Island, perhaps less than a mile. The first time nearly did me in as I huffed and puffed slow jogging a few yards, walking a longer distance, repeating the cycle, only too glad to reach the end. I felt awful. My feet hurt, legs felt like heavy logs, and lungs burned for air. I wanted to quit, give up for good, but that reminding voice, conscience, said I had made a commitment and had to stick with the pain, sweat and all.

With that decision hurdle over, I began jogging with jeans and sweatshirt but found them too heavy and hot. It had to be running shorts and T-shirt, which I had purposely avoided because of my fatness. I was too embarrassed to shop for them, but after looking through the stores as discreetly as possible, I finally found two pairs of men's shorts which fit, a trial-error purchase. No way was I going to ask to try them on in the fitting room, but if it didn't fit, it went into the Salvation Army bag. There was a paucity of extra-large sizes, which didn't always fit, so was glad whenever I found one. The one thing I was glad for was no one would know I wore men's shorts. I guess the manufacturers wised up because it wasn't too long after that unisex apparel of all sizes appeared, or perhaps, the stores experienced increased demand for large sizes for women. The top I decided on was a baseball shirt with three-quarter sleeves to protect my arms from the sun. Its length ended around my hips, but it felt heavy when wet with perspiration, so I cut it shorter to just reach my waist.

Now I was ready to do some serious jogging, but wait, I needed a hat to shade my face from the sun, one with a wide enough brim. I looked at straw hats but couldn't find anything that would allow air to breeze through the crown and fit my large head. One day I looked at my coconut hat in the bedroom and noticed its loose weave and wide brim, which held its shape well, a perfect jogging hat. The only problem was, because of its loose weave, it didn't fit snugly on my head and flew off with the wind, but wearing a sweatband solved that. The loose weave was also a plus when I pulled it down to just above my eyes because it gave me a clear view of traffic, runners, and cars through the brim without excessive head movement.

I stayed with the group for a while, always the last one to finish, but the important thing was I stuck with it until finally graduating to the Diamond Head path. Some called my jog a moderately paced walk and encouraged me to pick up speed. They didn't understand my slow pace and asked if I didn't feel more tired going so slow. No, but how could I know when I couldn't run fast without my lungs fizzing out. On one occasion some young men in a passing car, stuck their heads out and shouted, "faster, faster, too slow!" as I was going uphill. I yelled back, "Aw, shut up!" and muttered, "jerks!" as I struggled on. I was a definite plodder, my **choice,** because going faster taxed my breathing. True, it was a turtle's pace but comfortable for me, a "talk test" pace advised by Dr.

Jack Scaff, who conducted Sunday's Honolulu Marathon Clinic at Kapi'olani Park. He frequently reminded us that the right pace for each was to be able to talk while running. Another reminder was to hydrate well during a run, advice I took to heart. Water, that all important physical and spiritual source of life helped me to maintain a physiological balance.

I continued my slow jog, a pace my brother called "slogging", passed by many, content with the solitude it gave me to sort my thoughts as I competed with myself not others. It took time and lots of practice before I was able to increase the distance without tiring. In fact, I began to feel very good after jogging: calm, relaxed, and purged of my inner garbage. Although insomnia wasn't a problem, the moderate exercise brought sleep soon as my head hit the pillow to enjoy a restful night. The exercise helped me most after a stressful workday, making problems smaller and enabling a better perspective with clearer vision and understanding. It helped me gain a better attitude to accept the differences I encountered or saw in others and myself, and as I changed, the better my life.

That good feeling, I suppose could be called "runner's high", was the benefit of exercise and was probably responsible for my committing to do the Honolulu Marathon. It was a solid yes, do it, on my part. I knew that I couldn't entertain *any* doubt in completing twenty-six and two tenths miles. This was another big decision that told me I was standing, literally, on my own two feet, not on another's.

Marathon training, no small feat, lasted ten months with the Honolulu Marathon Clinic as my guide. It was a long and dedicated commitment of considerable time and energy. It was energy expended at least three times a week, and as the marathon drew near, four times a week for a weekly total of thirty or more miles. A day's rest in between gave muscles time to recoup. For many runners, thirty was a pittance, but to me, it was a big deal. My longest run was early Sunday morning when I did ten to fourteen miles. My time? Fifteen-minute miles.

Slow indeed, but it brought me humor whenever I met a runner who, when discovering I jogged and asked, with interest, my time, suddenly changed his or her demeanor to a mere "oh." Sometimes I saw the "ouch" on their faces. Notably, the women were more kind toward a slow time than men, who seemed to have been psychologically well conditioned for competition, while women, especially those my size, thought it was great. Serious men and women runners valued time as their "personal best", while for others like me, "personal best" meant committing and completing a never before thought of endeavor. The differing perspectives formed different attitudes.

It was only after I had begun training, I fully respected and admired the many runners who put in many more miles than I. It was through personal experience I understood the long-term commitment and discipline required to accomplish a "personal best." It's the same kind of commitment many of us apply to other undertakings be it home, business, or social.

It uses the same kind of energy and calls up the same kind of feelings—challenge, pain, and satisfaction. It also affirmed that experience is practice, a must for true learning, and that practice is a lifelong endeavor.

For me, personal best was just getting out there and plodding the distance. I had accepted myself as a plodder, but commitment was the important **choice** and impetus for follow through. It was, still is, and always will be important. How else would I complete any task?

Practicing for a marathon is a must. The Marathon Clinic repeatedly reminded us to train sensibly by gradually increasing mileage over a period of time and not hastily overload with miles. The staff often warned of potential injuries from over-training but stressed the need to run longer distances as we conditioned ourselves. It was this conditioning which would see us through those grueling twenty-six miles.

Sure, there were days I didn't feel like jogging, but I knew that if I did not, I'd regret it besides breaking the rhythm of a routine. Rhythm is an important part of daily living because it helps me to maintain a sense of balance. Our bodies function with rhythm and so does our universe.

When rhythm is interrupted, imbalance occurs something, I'm certain, we've all experienced when we say, "today must be my off day" or "nothing's going right."

I believe that imbalance causes not only our illnesses, but also the natural disasters on Earth. It's the same as saying we and our world are at dis-ease. What causes imbalance? Our thoughts, which, when combined, travel together with such force, to cause changes in our lives, our world. Thoughts are energy and "Thots are things", that ever-present reminder that what I think *does* make a difference, so I consciously practice and think the best. As said before, it doesn't mean I can't see when my best or that of others isn't being expressed. I am an imperfect being striving for perfection, but what's important is to keep practicing and become better in all the ways I know how no matter how limited my knowledge. Practice leads to perfection, that ultimate reality called **LOVE**.

At last, after practicing many months, the day of reckoning arrived, the big unknown test to tell me if training was adequate for completion. I had no clue as to what would happen, and although I had heard many others, including my brother, tell me of their experiences, I still couldn't fathom how I would feel.

Logistically, the marathon, manned by many well-wishing volunteers, was well planned for the thousands of runners placed into groups by predicted times. Certainly, not all remained in assigned areas, but no matter. There was tremendous excitement in the air with most smiling as they conversed with friends or strangers while a few were serious and introspective. With apparent camaraderie, I had no doubt that many new friendships began that day. The thousands of conversations melded into one deep prolonged sound until the countdown when the sudden silence signaled all to join the countdown in unison. The electrifying and intense force of energy increased until the gun went off followed by a tremendous roar as the runners left the starting line. It was a sea of people each with one goal in mind—to complete the race with their best time.

While I maintained my even turtle's pace, most passed me, but I kept my focus on placing one foot in front of the other and visualized each point I would reach, few miles at a time. It was after the half-way mark, I began to pass those who had slowed to a painful walk. I continued my slow jog until past the eighteenth mile, when I began to feel tired and sore all over. My feet hurt so much they didn't feel part of me, but the pain definitely did. Reaching the twentieth, I had to slow down to intermittent walk and jog. I was hot, tired, and sore, ready to give up. "Why am I punishing myself? What possessed me to stupidly pick this challenge? Never again!" The pick-up vehicle for those too tired or injured looked inviting, and their offer for a ride was tempting, but no way was I giving up when the end was near. Although I knew I was almost there, there was much self-talk going on to convince my body to continue. The pain in the bottom of my feet was unbearable, and so was the pressure of the shoelaces, though loosened. It was painful commitment and sheer will to remain focused on placing one foot in front of the other until I saw the banner, FINISH! It was that marvelous sight, which miraculously expelled the pain as I crossed that line with a broad smile.

My time? Over seven hours, but that didn't matter because I completed it and would have been deceiving myself if I had also included time. I was tired but elated with that **choice**, a decision for something I had never done or imagined possible, a truly incredible feat for me—a feat without major injury. Another outcome I understood and appreciated after the race was the importance of long-distance training—practice.

Without doubt, long runs were necessary to build stamina and conditioning to last distance while speed came later. Practice or training does make perfect.

The marathon experience was a reminder that I was practicing to live, no different than other experiences I have had or tasks I do daily. It also was another lesson to understand that preparation would help me with the future. It taught me to see training as practice, practice as experience, experience as a lesson and lesson as training to bring me to knowing and action—the circle of life full of daily lessons *if* I look for it.

The day after the marathon was continuation of pain. My body ached some, but my legs hurt more, much more. They were stiff, inflexible boards, paining with every twitch and movement as I slowly went about readying for work. The day before I had thought of staying home day after the marathon, but it wasn't a serious option and didn't really think about it after. As I painfully made my way to the door, I had no idea how much more was in store until that first step down. My knee buckled on that step, thigh too sore to support body weight, forcing me to use the railing for support. "Great, how am I gonna get down the forty steps? Step at a time, how else, and use the rail as your support." It took a while, but I finally made it to the car and somehow maneuvered into the seat. Once in, it wasn't too bad to shift since I didn't have to change leg position too often.

Once at work, my boss watched me grimace as I moved slowly and stiffly about. He smiled and shook his head wondering aloud why people punished themselves with so much pain. Where there were steps there was pain, but the day ended with a most pleasant surprise. My fellow joggers/runners presented me with a small carved wooden dish with the words, "MOST ENDURANCE", a cherished trophy. They were right, it took sheer will to endure and complete my first marathon in over seven hours, my "personal best" and I was proud of it!

Was it my first and last marathon? Nope. How quickly I had forgotten the pain, time, and energy it took to train and complete that first one. I entered and completed three more with similar times but was happy with them and accepted myself as I was. It was more important to **choose** i.e. make a decision and act on it. I was practicing commitment and follow through, and yes, *living* by the challenges I **chose**.

Did I lose weight? About ten pounds, a small amount when compared to the forty plus I needed to lose. Slow weight loss came when I jogged a minimum of twenty-five miles and curbed my food intake. I wasn't ready to consume less, but the exercise definitely gave me more vigor and vitality. It was only after the first two marathons I realized that jogging is great for physical conditioning but wasn't the answer to controlling weight. As someone once said to me, one good exercise for weight loss is to push away from the table, all things in moderation, and good nutrition was definitely in.

Purging inner garbage was my major benefit from jogging, and because of it, I was willing to sacrifice personal time and energy. It was another example of having to make a sacrifice for whatever I wanted, desired. It helped me to understand better that all desires required a giving up of some kind. It's these same wants which reveal our values for living.

Jogging also was a reminder that I am totally responsible for my health that I was born with this body so must care for it, and that it houses my spirit, the essence of my soul. I can seek medical services when I deem them necessary, but the healing and abuses are *my* **choices**. I can say, "Doctor, help me", if I am ill or injure myself, but I cannot blame him if I don't follow his prescription. His responsibility is to render his best knowledge and service and mine is to follow as I believe, envisioning a healthy me—a cooperative effort i.e. he renders and I do, but not blindly.

Still another lesson was the realization of a desire, that is, if I really wanted to do something, I could do it. I could do it because I *believed* in myself—faith in self. With faith in self I can have faith in others—belief and trust. This was a lesson from long ago, but I had to re-learn it many more times before it began to sink in. "Thots are things" are desires when coupled with faith, a belief that with the Ultimate Source all things are possible, can become. I believe we all come from the same Universal Source, Allah, God, so doesn't that mean we have godlike traits within us, hidden until we **choose** to reveal them to ourselves? And in **choosing**, manifest them by thought, word, and deed?

XV

GOD WITHIN

*G*od within. What does it mean? I had heard and read it many times, but I couldn't grasp an understanding. It seemed that I had read many writings, listened to many ministers, priests, and people speak of their understanding of God and had reflected upon them forever without success. I had read that we're from God, and therefore, are gods. Are we?

Since I am from God and am god also, it makes a lot of sense to me that, as god, all things are possible. Whatever I visualize happening can happen if I truly desire and believe it will, "thots are things." I believe that for "it" to happen, the desire must not harbor greed or malice. Why? Because what goes around, comes around—karma; you reap what you sow, harvest what you plant. God, Allah, the Universal Consciousness or whichever label I **choose** is **LOVE**, the ultimate reality of all there is— perfection. **LOVE** is that special light within all of us, awaiting discovery, an open door to show itself in all we think, feel, and do.

Many of us seek love outside of ourselves from people, places, and things as we explicitly or implicitly state we seek happiness, to be happy. I see it as a desire to be loved through understanding and acceptance and through thoughts, words, and deeds. We want and expect others to make us happy, and when they fail in our eyes for whatever reasons, we blame them for our unhappy state. We relinquish responsibility for our life by placing our expectations upon others.

I wanted to be happy too, perfect and happy but was reminded frequently in different ways that I was imperfect. Whenever everything went well, I was happily filled with satisfaction that I had done everything "right" then something would happen, bursting that bubble. It was a rude awakening to discover that I was filled with selfish thoughts without consideration for or communication with others. I didn't understand that love, that unconditional giving, *is* perfection. Perhaps even now I haven't fully grasped its meaning, but I do understand and believe that it is the most or close to the most powerful energy force. I can't prove it, but my ever-present inner feeling, intuition, tells me it is. I am listening to and trusting my inner more, not someone else's.

When told in various ways that I was imperfect, I became judge and jury and **chose** to accept others' perceptions of me. I also delved in self-criticism, was my harshest judge until I had little love for self, feeling more down than up. Goodness, if I couldn't love myself, how could I love another or expect them to love me? In judging myself, I judged others and in judging others, I judged myself—a circle in perpetual motion. At times I joined them in cynical criticism with thought or word. Even if I didn't verbalize hurtful criticism, the deed was done. Thoughts are deeds because thinking is the same as doing. "Thots are things", making us part of each other and of all around us.

When I began to love myself again, I could look forward to living this life with confidence. I'm not saying that I was void of self-love. I did love myself though not unconditionally, i.e. all the pluses and minuses, for by not admitting my negatives, how could I accept all of me?

My parents loved me unconditionally, giving much love without strings attached and without finding fault or heavy restrictions, but it was the in-between times when siblings labeled me bratty that instilled doubts. That label became a self-fulfilling prophecy as I took on the role, to the hilt at times, which caused me to travel uphill. I could have made life easier, but I **chose** the more trying path by being obnoxious. Does not overcoming a harder test make one stronger and better? On the other hand, I can't say that taking the path of least resistance wouldn't have had the same results.

My parents and siblings were my first teachers. They taught me that love isn't always a bed of roses, that it can be a school of hard knocks even for a child. A school that develops strength not muscle, courage not doubt, and action not wishful thinking, to stand on one's own two feet.

Love isn't always hugs and kisses. It manifests itself by anger, frustration from a parent, sibling, spouse, or friend to one he/she loves, or by alienation and isolation to allow time, space to learn. My parents' love allowed me to be the child I was, and my siblings' love was through the strict discipline they enforced whenever I was lax. They rarely let me be my usual lazy self by keeping me busy under their watchful eyes, correcting me if wrong, and insisting I repeat tasks when sloppy. They had an uncanny sense of discovering when I cheated in doing chores. When assigned to a redo, they reminded me not to grumble, my favorite reaction, when I thought they couldn't hear me. I grumbled so often, one sister called me Fujinaga, the grumbler. That label stuck so well, my aunt gave me a Grumpy doll from Snow White and the Seven Dwarves for Christmas, a hurtful gift.

I may have been a child, but children have feelings too. What adults see as harmless humor may indeed be harmful. I can't say I was greatly hurt, but I thought she was a nice person and really liked her, so was hurt and disappointed that she had agreed with my sister.

Now I see her gift as an expression of her love for me. She was telling me something with that doll, giving me feedback that perhaps I needed to affect change in my attitude, my life. She must have wanted me to see where I was and what I was doing to myself, but I think it would have better if she had explained her intent. My problem then was youthful shortsightedness and inability to accept that non-verbal feedback, but because I couldn't understand why she, a kind and thoughtful person would hurt me, I tucked it in the back of my mind to remember and learn from when time. Sometimes we internalize and carry garbage around for almost a lifetime only to discover how a changed perspective brings understanding and acceptance, the key to letting go as life goes on.

XVI

DEALING WITH THE ECONOMY

*I*t seemed that I had just settled into work and home when I had to think of coming up with the balloon or balance of the principal payment for the house. One year remained on the agreement of sale, time to begin searching for a home loan, and although I felt my income wouldn't qualify, I had hoped for decreasing mortgage rates. Hoping turned to worry as inflation pushed rates to double digits, an economic situation, often in the news, which affected so many. It was a dilemma for me because reading articles that a major criterion to qualify was the ratio of three or four to one for monthly income to payment diminished optimism. It was time to research available options regardless of the discouraging news. I still hoped that somewhere, somehow, someone would be able to assist me. I started with the neighborhood bank, the largest in our State, only because the credit union I belonged to didn't do home loans. I knew the answer would be no but had to know for certain. It was interesting how polite, tactful, and business-like the bank employee was, especially since she had been so friendly on my prior visits to the bank often asking about family. She was the first and only contact I had for a loan and wasn't interested on how we were doing, only interested in conveying a no in her most polite manner.

The change was noticeable, and I was perplexed. Perhaps it was due to employer training, but whatever triggered it was immaterial because she **chose** to change. Which was her *real* self—the friendly, interested in your family, or the tactful, slow-soft-speaking-choosing-words-carefully one, or yet another. I couldn't tell, but no matter, I only wanted to hear the bank's answer. She told me that my income didn't meet the bank's requirement of four to one. My income was barely one-half of the requirement, and although I foresaw the answer, it still was discouraging to see the largest bank in the State, make money from so many little people and practice caution and inflexibility, unwilling to take any risk on those same people. Having very good credit didn't matter—that rule didn't have the flexibility of bamboo, but it was okay, because I took my money out and banked it in a credit union, a practice I adhere to this day. Now, it amuses me to receive unsolicited offers of pre-approved platinum charge cards from local banks in town—baby, how your tune has changed!

Anyway, I was hopeful that somewhere I would meet someone who would say, "Yes, you qualify." The second contact was with the owner, thinking that, just perhaps, he would extend the agreement of sale for another year. I called and related the bank's decision and asked if he'd consider an extension. Instead of a direct no, he said he needed the money for his business. It was the Asian way of saying no, and at the same time telling me that I must find financing. Strangely, I was annoyed. I had lived on the mainland so long amongst direct speaking people, I had buried that part of my culture—conveying a message within a message and as tactfully as possible. Is that inscrutability? If so, can't say only Asians do it. He gave his reason and had every right to want his pay-out.

I had signed, he had waited, and it was time to honor the agreement.

Is a message within a message, inscrutable, mysterious? I only understand it sometimes. I smile now when I think of the many times I thought I understood my father only to find out later I didn't. I remember the times he would listen to me and with few words or questions, without revealing a solution or opinion, allow me to think, stretch my mind. It was just one of his teaching methods to help me stand on my own two feet.

Other times he'd ask questions just to see where my head was or what personal value I held.

One day after my Junior High friends had left, he asked how come I had such funny looking friends. I was offended and told him they weren't funny looking, and that I picked friends not for their looks but for their inner goodness. It was years later, during reflective moments, I realized he was checking out my personal values. This is just one important reason for meditation or moments alone—to have fond remembrances of life's lessons and love.

It was really disappointing to have both the bank and owner say no, but a few days later, the owner called and said that he had thought it over and was willing to extend the agreement of sale at, of course, a higher rate. Immediately, I had the sense that he hadn't been totally honest when he said he needed the money right away. With the sudden and surprising change of mind, his motive, probably the double-digit rates in effect, became suspect, so I declined the offer. It would have been better if he had been up-front, but no matter because my inner said to look for another lender in town.

Armed only with a sense of optimism, my next step was to call a mortgage lender for an appointment. The gentleman I met with asked all the financially pertinent information regarding assets and liabilities. As I watched his fingers nimbly running over the calculator keys and intermittently referring to well-worn pages in his little book of numbers, I was almost afraid to breathe for fear of disturbing his concentration and rhythm. Surprisingly the wait was relatively shorter than expected, less than twenty minutes. I held my breath for the verdict as he slowly put his pen down, looked seriously at me, and announced that I qualified for an FHA loan, a conclusion without fanfare, handshake, or congratulations that I had made it.

It was a strictly business process, a matter-of-fact interaction, but a joyous miracle, heaven's answer to my thoughts and prayers, and the best news received in a very long time. I was curious and asked why I was able to qualify. He explained that FHA income requirements were lower than banks, a simple answer gratefully received. With a satisfied, elated, and "do it now" feeling, I asked him to begin the loan process right away.

Applying for a home loan was another lesson in living. It was a lesson in economics, that social science which encompasses financing, human values, emotions, and our environment. At the time of my application, the only financing I knew was a signed agreement to repay an agreed upon sum in a timely manner. This time I learned more—points, amortized payments, escrow, and the various services used in processing home loans. I learned from questions asked and from newspaper articles on financing, especially home mortgages. Because of high interest rates, there were many articles to teach me terminology, processes, how to save on interest, etc. The interesting result of the articles is that I had more questions, and not too long after thinking of them, there were other articles with answers—thots are things!" One valuable money management lesson was pre-paying principal to reduce the total interest paid by remitting the next month's principal with the current month's payment of interest and principal. Pre-paying the next month's principal "saved" its interest i.e. interest would not be paid, and if the same payment schedule continued each month, the house would be paid in half the time—fifteen years. What was needed was an amortization schedule, which listed the dates with exact principal and interest amounts and usually was sent free upon request. That was then. Now, in addition to thirty-year mortgages there are fifteen-year and even variable rate financing. Lenders have become creative to remain viable.

There had been enough written articles on how much more above the principal we pay for a home, but I didn't know the thousands involved until I received my schedule. I was flabbergasted at how much larger the interest was compared to principal with beginning payments largely interest, decreasing until the last payment while the reverse was true for principal. No wonder buying a home is a big and expensive decision and practically a lifetime commitment.

That information prompted me to pay for more than several months principal and continue long as I could. It was good to know that I didn't have to pay those months' interest and reduced principal more quickly toward independence, but even with prepayments, the balance decreased slower than I wanted. As a side note, it wasn't advised to prepay principal if one plans to move in a few years. No point in tying up money in real estate which is less liquid during slow times.

What I learned about mortgage financing piqued my interest in learning more about the business aspect of living. With encouragement from my sister-in-law, who worked for H&R Block on the mainland, I decided it was time to learn how our tax system worked. I thought why not, after all, nearly everyone pays taxes, and it was a good starting point for learning. Another reason was the CPA, who prepared my tax returns with annual fee increases although forms and info remained the same. It was time to change.

I enrolled in H&R Block's Level One tax course and was amazed at the information acquired, pointing out my total ignorance. There is no mysticism in tax preparation, but the myriad of information and wordiness could easily become overwhelming. Careful reading and study is a must for understanding legalese especially when tax laws change and cause confusion when wording is unclear, initiating complaints to the Internal Revenue Service.

Other courses followed the next few years, but as a firstimer, the first course was the best. From it I learned that points for a mortgage loan was deductible when paid out-of-pocket, a revelation which allowed me to amend my return for a refund of more than two hundred dollars. The amount was a lot for me but more important was the knowledge and ability to do it, telling me that being informed helps to stand on my two feet better.

During other courses from Block, I realized how ignorant I was of money matters and began subscribing to business magazines, reading the financial pages in the evening paper, and taking an evening course in stock investing. Following that course, I could read the Wall Street Journal with better understanding, but still felt I was missing something, that there was something else to learn.

The one thing I became aware of was the phrase "economists predict" such and such. Who were they, what did they do, and how do they predict? Was prediction a psychic process or was it based on fact and which ones? So many questions, no answers, so decided to enroll in macro and microeconomics at the University of Hawai'i for a letter grade. The **choice** for a grade was a recheck to see if my learning cells were functional. They were. I enjoyed the courses, which instilled an enthusiasm and further interest to take another econ course, money and banking. I found it difficult yet revealing of how our money system works—controlled.

I didn't know what I was to see or learn from the three courses, but it did broaden my sight and better understanding—perspective. It confirmed, for me, that all organizations, including non-profit ones, have an economic base. How else could they survive? Staff must be paid, supplies purchased, rent paid, etc. It was one of the first things I learned as a graduate student in health planning. Health care is also a business, very big business.

Big business, a term, to me, which signifies high demand by consumers or corporations which have little or almost no competition, and therefore, dealing with millions or even billions of dollars. It's competition for a piece of the money pie by those with creative strategies, and or products and services that create big business. Many begin small while a few become giants, absorbing or deleting the smaller businesses through whatever means. Consumers, that is, individuals, groups or other businesses, are buyers of the goods and services offered, and therefore, as my economic professor said, "grease the economy." Within the consumer group are the paid workers who hold businesses together with their skills, abilities, and talents. The Federal Reserve banks and Board of Governors serve as hub of the economic wheel, extending their spokes and policies, to strengthen and stabilize the wheel. I see the Board, composed of seven members, including a chairman nominated by our President and approved by the Senate, as a powerful, elite group whose monetary policy controls interest rates, money supply, and us.

The one disturbing item I learned was our money supply has no gold backing, a decision during Richard Nixon's tenure. Why does it disturb me? Since the Federal Reserve Board determines money supply, does it mean that when more money is needed, more is printed at the say so of a few? What holds up its value? Faith? Why not? Is not faith the backbone of our decisions and actions? Is not faith our belief system that what we do is right for us, that we will not fail, that we can and will overcome hardships or barriers in our paths?

I see faith as an outgrowth from love, for it is love that gives us the will to persevere as we journey on. To have faith is to believe that something is or will be. It is unshakable even under extreme duress. I see faith as mankind's prime mover for survival. It is the mover of peoples and builder of nations. It is that indescribable and inexplicable force of the universe that gives me the will to live again. It is faith, that glimmer of hope, that tells me all things happen for a reason, that patience is a virtue but does not mean apathy, and that a problem does not exist forever and that darkness is not always unkind. It tells me to believe that I am god and all things become possible, to love myself and love for others will follow, and to strengthen my inner which takes care of the outer.

I still feel a bit uncomfortable with the thought of a few experts controlling the nation's monetary system but accept what is for now. What I had learned brought some understanding to the why of double digit interest rates. I didn't like the Board's decision, but I reminded myself that I had **chosen** to be ignorant of the world I lived in, so was responsible for my own ignorance, but I could **choose** not to remain passive. Now I know that what happens elsewhere does affect me, us. All that happens on Earth affects us. We are but parts of the whole, so what we think, feel, and do *does* make a difference.

XVII

MAKING A DIFFERNCE

*M*aking a difference. How does one make a difference on Earth? I can only make a difference where I am, if I so **choose**. To me, and am certain to many others, making a difference is making ourselves better so we can assist others to do the same, and it doesn't mean we can't do it together, as Stephen Covey states, for a win-win situation for all. How do I make things better? By following through with what I feel I must or should do. How do I know what and when? Again, by listening to my inner feeling and knowing that same gut feeling which tells and prods me to do it.

The one situation I remember well is when I **chose** to counter my supervisor for what I felt was an oppressive work situation. If I did nothing, my situation wouldn't improve and thus be my responsibility.

The risk was losing my job though some would say that it's difficult to fire a government worker, but it could have happened.

As I've mentioned before, the health plan association where I had been working practiced cost containment wages, similar to banks and insurance companies, and with increased mortgage rates, I had to either find a higher paying position or get a second job. I still vividly remembered the stress of working at two jobs, so scratched that thought.

Administrative positions weren't easy to come by with the interesting ones requiring more experience in budgeting and personnel than I had, but I applied anyway. I also applied for a clinical laboratory technologist position with the military hospital not knowing I'd soon be hired sight unseen.

It was another first for me being hired without a look-see and interview, a discomfort zone, so contacted the officer in charge and requested one. His voice sounded calm and pleasant enough, an indication that he may not be prone to episodic spasms. It was much later I learned the reason for no interview—a 10-point veteran's preference which I had applied for as a veteran's widow. It seemed a strong justification was required for refusing to hire, and since there was none, it was meant to be.

As I entered the major's office for the interview, I saw a woman in white uniform sitting next to him. She was the section supervisor. One look at her face with narrowed eyes told me that I wasn't welcome, that she preferred I had refused the job. What I saw upon entering was confirmed during our conversation when the major asked if she had anything to add. She must have been busy preparing her speech because she quickly verbalized her thoughts. She informed me that the workload was tremendous and was, in fact, like a very busy production line. She said she wanted to make certain I was aware of how it was before I started and re-emphasized how busy they were.

I sensed her hope of discouraging me enough to refuse the position, but I've never been afraid of work and had no thought of a cushy job. Perhaps she would have preferred an easier job at her age, but I still had a lot of life in me. I told her I knew it was very busy because I had interned there and didn't think the workload had diminished. Her eyes widened in surprise as she said, "I didn't know you interned here.

You didn't have that on your application". My reply, "There's nothing in the application that asked where I interned. Besides, I didn't think it mattered", elicited a displeased, suspicious look. I'm certain she viewed me as a problem, but the problem was her thought.

A med tech friend, whom I trusted then but who broke that trust later, heard that I had accepted the job and called me to say the supervisor was "no good" and didn't look out for or supported her staff. While listening, I appreciated the information but already had had a feeling it would not be a bed of roses. So, why take a job with a bumpy road?

Simple, my priority was maximizing my earnings to keep a roof over my family, a basic need. I felt I could handle working with a lousy supervisor, and optimistically, she may not be so bad after all. I'd rather think the best of others, and since my perceptions sometimes differed from others, although I appreciated their help, I almost always **chose** to find out for myself. In that way, I did my own research, applied my own value system, and thus, was responsible for my own bias.

Going to work at that hospital was like returning to the point of origin as a medical technologist because it was where I had interned during my last twelve months of college before entering the "real world" of work. The twelve months involved much practical on-the-job training with theoretical application. It prepared me to not only perform various laboratory procedures with care, accuracy, and dexterity, but also to plan and organize work-flow efficiently. It was working full-time without compensation, but the knowledge and practice gained, served me well through time.

The major was nice enough with administrative responsibilities taking him out from the lab most of the time, while the supervisor was our liaison with whomever or for whatever, made assignments, approved leave, and most important to many, evaluated us.

It wasn't long after I began to see the stresses affecting people. While the tremendous work volume played a large part, the rest appeared to be due to people themselves. Some were overly reactive to work or people situations, stressing themselves; some appeared cool, calm, collected but unhappy within, by their occasional comments; a few worked quietly, saying little; while less than few voiced their opinions or questioned decisions. It was a chop-suey mix of personalities with most being afraid or feeling nothing gained by interacting with or talking with her. The fear of reprisal during evaluations seemed to hang over most.

Work assignments to the various areas were arbitrarily set with no sense of a patterned rotation. The less stressful sections were given to her nice and cooperative "friends", who didn't question her decisions. It became evident that I wasn't in the chosen group and, consequently, was rotated between the two busiest areas. I didn't fault any one for that situation because I was and am the maker of my own destiny.

After a few months, she came to me in her nicest manner, stating her dilemma in scheduling assignments. She needed someone to cover the busiest section and asked if I would mind doing it. I told her I didn't and would work wherever assigned. I knew that in saying that I opened the door wide, giving her free rein for probable harassment.

Fellow workers so much as told me my consent was a mistake, but isn't a mistake a **choice** and a lesson? They felt I should have refused and requested another section, and I somewhat agreed, but was curious as to how long she'd keep me in those areas—about two years. When I felt I had stagnated in the same areas long enough, I requested the special procedures section. It was only honored after a long time had passed with excuses. I was still being assigned to the undesirable, stress-ridden sections. It seemed that since she couldn't discourage me from first accepting the position, she was attempting to pour the work on so I'd get disenchanted enough to quit.

After approximately two years, I decided to do something. Why did I wait so long? As an optimist, I was hopeful the situation would improve. I also knew that I'd be "rocking the boat", and like many others, didn't want to cause "trouble". Taking what comes without "making trouble" seems to be a local trait, perhaps, as a friend once said to me, a plantation mentality when workers did what the luna (Hawaiian for supervisor) ordered, and perhaps, a part of the Asian culture. Regardless of the origin, many years of conditioning still influenced thinking and behavior.

It was only after much time and considerable thought I knew that, if I didn't do anything, my situation wouldn't change; that it was time to take a "risk"; that it was time for "feedback". I often recalled Bill G. and Jerry G. from graduate school speaking of taking a risk to find out what will work and giving or taking "feedback" by word or deed to see what wavelength we're on. Of course, it must be accompanied with thought, i.e. without malice or deliberate attempt to hurt and destroy.

She always approached me cordially though cautiously, like a wary cat watching my every move, uncertain of my mood or reaction, but whenever I agreed to do what she wanted, her body relaxed. Her approach always seemed well planned and rehearsed yet I sensed her uneasiness. Was it fear? Several techs told me that since my manner and words were without fear of her, she was somewhat afraid of me, and therefore, spoke "nicer" to me than them. If indeed she was afraid, I related to it because I was still working out my fears—if she only knew.

It was after such feedback I realized that I had acquired the ability to pick and say things from the top of my head. Sometimes, I even surprised myself at what I said or how I expressed myself, and found that, when I articulated what I truly felt within, thoughts and words flowed freely. How come? I like to think it's because I stopped worrying about what others thought of me and focused on being honest with myself which naturally extended to others.

I see it as confirmation that what we feel deep within is our true selves waiting to be recognized and accepted by self to freely emerge.

Our true self is without malice or fear, traits that change our exterior to doubt, hide, lie, cheat, or harm. True self is love, the Light of God, I see radiating from others and which can and will radiate from all.

As I discovered, I encouraged others to dispel their fears and regain courage to stand on their own two feet, but I knew that I could only persuade, not **choose** for them. In sharing, I not only was teaching just as they shared and taught me but was taking a risk to practice what I preached. The risk was not knowing what would happen—the consequence.

Unbeknownst to me, teaching was fulfilling my need, purpose in life, showing and sharing lessons in living, a path I had **chosen** so long ago. I should have known when my children, while in grade school, told me I would make a good teacher and wished I was theirs, but neither they nor I could see I was and would be a good part of their lives.

Because we're teachers and students to each other, we can't lock ourselves into any one role, a pigeon-hole. It's not living. Self-limitation only strengthens and perpetuates inflexibility, stunting growth and progress. That is what I have learned from a supervisor who took her role to heart and believed she *had* to maintain control over us, much like a parent who believes in controlling their children. With this understanding, I could accept her, knowing full well that we all grow further when it is time. I also embraced more the understanding that each of us is the cause of the effects we encounter in life. Karma: we reap what we sow; we harvest what we plant.

I felt the stresses of work. Quite often, as she spoke, I visualized her sitting at her desk thinking of ways to make my work life stressful, to retaliate for whatever reason. It was no secret, as I was told, that I had earned the label of "trouble-maker" and so too those who **chose** to keep company with me. I saw that label distanced most of the others from me with a few sitting on the fence, appearing uninvolved, but on occasion, when they saw a probable, not possible, benefit for themselves, temporarily drew closer. No matter, such was their way of living—*their* **choice**.

Did I make a difference? Probably, because there was behavior modification toward me but not to others, although there was another spunky person who voiced her thoughts. Other techs said the supervisor was her usual intimidating self to them, and two told me the complaint only made her more cautious, not better. By then, I had already decided that if they wanted to affect change, they had to be part of the whole process, not sit back while others did not, and come forth only when they felt it was safe.

Risk-taking obviously isn't for everyone and is often dependent on perceived consequences, i.e. some go only as far as their comfort zone while others go beyond, all degrees requiring courage. It isn't always simple and easy to leave our comfort zone, that usual predictable and acceptable place, into the unpredictable unknown. Nonetheless, we all seem to be working on personal courage to enable facing that space outside of ourselves—the unknown.

Jogging made risk-taking less stressful and I thank God for it. It played a major role in helping to maintain inner calm and made tolerable the arbitrary work assignments, non-selection for additional training, and general treatment that I was of little value. The only plus training I received was from the **choice** to become a volunteer EEO counselor. As a new civil service employee, I was curious as to the workings of government, and since things happen when it's time and for a reason, I couldn't help but feel this would be a good opportunity to learn much more—another gut feeling. I was ignorant of what the counselor's role would be but soon found out when various training classes were scheduled. Since complaints were usually against supervisors, training took me through two phases of supervisory classes, personnel classification and selection, research, conducting interviews, and much more. I began to understand the meaning of bureaucracy—long, formal processes (reminds me of publicized court cases), requiring lots of paper, time, energy, and of course, money. The process involved multiple levels, with diverse personalities, who sometimes saw fit to give confusing interpretations or emphasized their importance but were afraid of making any decision. I sometimes wondered if some weren't aware of their responsibilities, yet also found many civil servants who do know and work cohesively to keep our government going. I salute them!

Training as an EEO counselor showed the way to give feedback to my supervisor. It was the knowledge gained which gave me the means to do something about my work situation, but it was only after considerable agonized thought whether it was right for me. God knew I didn't want revenge but only wanted her to know I didn't like her treatment of people and to stop stepping on my toes. Certainly, I could have spoken directly with her, but when I attempted to do so with repeated phrases of "one can only control self, not another; it doesn't pay to take advantage or intimidate another because what goes around comes around, etc.", she didn't pick up on it. Speak directly with her? To do that a third party would have to be present, not one who'd change colors like a chameleon, and if I picked someone I trusted, I saw the bias accusation surfacing. She was basically a good person, but I didn't trust her actions.

By the time of the complaint, another officer was in charge. He had acquired a penchant for timing my fifteen-minute coffee breaks after the complaint had been filed. One day when another tech and I got off the elevator, a trifle slow for a hospital that could have housed fifteen hundred beds during World War II, we saw him standing in the hall with glaring eyes aimed at us. He made a perfect picture of the Chinese dragon with fierce red eyes, nostrils snorting steam, waiting to devour us. The difference was that the Chinese dragon represents a celestial being and he did not. As we entered the lab, he looked at his watch and walked into the supervisor's office. A tech in the office at the time informed us that our names were written as being five minutes late from morning break.

Oh, the games we play to make a minor point only after a complaint had been filed which told them their image wasn't so perfect, so documentation was the name of that game, a game many play today. After all, if it isn't written, it wasn't done, a symptom of fear based on financial, emotional, or physical liability—loss, or just because.

I knew the complaint would upset her world, but once I had decided, there was no turning back. My solution was to request an Organizational Effectiveness officer's review, an Army major at that time. I really wanted to request her removal from a supervisory role and zombie her into a non-supervisor's position where she would have no say over another but let her keep her civil service grade. I didn't ask for it because I saw great resistance, and after all, she seemed to have the support of the military heads who probably didn't want to go through the hassle of paper work. If possible, we all look for the path of least resistance.

One day she called me into the department head's office for a private conversation. She began with, "Soo, I intend to keep my job and work for a long time." I was surprised because it seemed to infer that I coveted her supervisor's position. It was an inference confirmed several years later when I became lab supervisor with the Navy after which she congratulated me for "finally getting what" I "wanted." This was just one of those times I didn't get immediate confirmation of what I saw beneath the obvious surface until much later.

There was no point in denying that motive because she wouldn't have believed me—*her* **choice**. I bore no malice or devious plan for her position, and I certainly didn't want her to be out of work. I wanted our work environment, a place where we spent at least eight and a half hours daily, to be better, and the first step could have been letting people know they had worth. She could have helped in building a more trusting climate and not allow fear to creep in and perpetuate it with punitive measures—a somewhat prevailing trait of the military.

What was the outcome of the complaint? In the minds of most of the techs, nothing, but in mine, a lot—just a matter of perspective. She didn't fully share the OE officer's review and acted as though things were okay, but it didn't matter because I saw her fear. I knew she wouldn't follow through, as confirmed by the officer when some techs spoke with him. They told me about it as if I should go into action, but what I wanted to do was done.

I saw fear as the major reason for her pretense that everything was okay. I related well with that same fear—fear of job loss or poor work evaluation, of repercussion or abuse, of losing life's savings, of dying—so many fears of loss, blanketing life with darkness.

It was fear that made me value others' opinion of me—fear of losing my self-image, my identity. I see it as a lack of self-worth, self-love. It makes a lot of sense that when I love myself, it doesn't matter what others think of me. If they can't accept me as I am with all my faults, that's *their* **choice**. If I value their opinions, I couldn't become better in all ways because my expended energy would be for their approval. This doesn't mean that I don't need kudos for job well done, I, too, am receptive to positive feedback. I would do the same for anyone even my boss. I do not apologize for who I am. I am what I am. I can only be what I feel I must be, and that, I believe, is *my* **choice**.

The techs believed that change would not come, and although I was uncertain, I couldn't help but feel deep down that it would come— slowly. Why? Because life is dynamic, not a standstill. I also knew that the time for change depends on the scope and depth of the problems identified and the open willingness of all involved. We're all part of the problem and solution. The immediate change was a temporary respite from her frequent hovering and her hesitancy in approaching us. Perhaps it was my imagination, but I felt she was a bit nicer to all of us for a short time.

After that seemingly long EEO process which bore the conclusion of no age discrimination found, a non-surprise, I wondered how much longer I would remain. Almost from the beginning and after seeing the oppressive work environment, I looked for another job. I couldn't help but be amused at times in seeing myself trying so hard but unable to leave. I must have applied for a dozen management analyst positions, deemed qualified, but not selected. It became apparent that I was to remain longer than I wanted because I had **chosen** that test, lesson, for myself. It was another lesson to take charge of my life and do what I felt was right. It reminded me that, as an employee, I had a moral responsibility, an obligation, to better my work environment. Also, as a human being, I had that same obligation to better my whole life. It is in bettering my life I would be able to, with others, better all life. Call it working together, teaming for life.

A short time after, a friend called to say I should apply for a medical technician position where she worked. Since I had openly shared details of my work situation, she knew I was still looking and wanted me to apply. At last my "thot" was to become a 'thing', joyous news that the time had finally arrived for my departure, an indication that that lesson was finished. It was time for another.

The day I was notified of my selection, I immediately gave my supervisor notice. It was obvious that she was most pleased and so was the captain who came in with face and eyes oozing with delight, a stark contrast to the mustachioed tight lips, flared nostrils, and glaring eyes of EEO days. Even his mustache seemed to come alive with joy. From the first time I saw him, his appearance reminded me of an infamous European dictator and his manner that of a child who only saw so far. He may have a Ph.D. in chemistry, but he forgot to balance it with people skills.

Both congratulated me several times within a few minutes, and while they quickly had forgotten that I was taking a downgrade to technician, below a technologist, the few who saw that could only shake their heads. Obviously, the value of getting rid of their "trouble-maker" was more important for their peace of mind, an understandable **choice**.

They probably believed that once I was gone, things would be better for them, but I found out later it wasn't to be. New techs were hired, more complaints filed followed by her diminished responsibilities with sections separated, each with its own supervisor. The separation may or may not have been deliberately devised to diminish her power base, for it could have been for a more effective and efficient work-flow. Whatever the reason, I believe all happenings come when it is time.

XVIII

LEARNING TO MEDITATE

$\mathcal{T}$he environment of my next job at a Naval medical clinic was markedly different and a welcome change. The work volume was less and the stress nil, allowing more focus on things like exercise and other personal interests. After the job change, I decided to stop training for the marathon and reduce weekly mileage. Although I gained its benefits, I never did feel jogging was my kind of exercise, and with more articles on injuries, I decided to re-assess its continued value. I wasn't afraid of pain, but I was of permanent injury and felt that continuing constant impact would eventually lead to it. I was a slow jogger and didn't do much bouncing, but the frequent injury articles were my cue to stop and look for something else.

It was time to exercise my mind again, so enrolled in night classes at the University, but after taking three consecutive courses for letter grades, I felt mentally and physically burnt out. With studies consuming most of my spare time and energy, weekly jogging mileage dropped to twelve, six, or none accompanied with diminished energy. The lack of exercise and my continuing hearty appetite caused the Bulge to strike again only with more poundage than before. It was the same story of losing weight only to regain more than I had lost. I had a good self-image and couldn't see my obesity until I saw a family snapshot. My face was fully round with two and a half chins, and though smiling, my eyes were mere slits, and my body, well, rounder and more corpulent than before. I had focused so intently on strengthening my inner self, I had neglected my outer, that dispensable shell which houses my soul.

Seeking respite from academia, I decided to take a fun course, Tai Chi Chuan, a Chinese martial art which many use as exercise. I remembered taking it years ago but had stopped when my grade school daughter told me I wasn't spending enough time with her. I liked the slow, rhythmic movements, my kind of exercise, I thought, and delved into it further by learning the longer traditional Yang style. It gave me the same benefits as running plus more as I experienced a deeper sense of serenity similar to when swimming in the Pacific.

Soon after I began Tai Chi Chuan, I attended a meditation workshop presented by one of Honolulu's psychics. Having heard and read of its benefits, I was definitely interested, but my conditioned mother response of spending on family not self, caused a momentary hesitation. It was a hesitation from the many years dollars went for children's needs, and had to remind myself it was okay to spend on self that I was worth it.

There were many people at the workshop, well over a hundred and larger than I had expected. I sensed the eagerness and enthusiasm of the group, representing diversity in gender, age, and ethnicity. The group became quiet when the psychic appeared. She spoke briefly on the program then instructed us to get comfortable for meditation. She put on serenely pleasant New Age music, and as it played, we positioned ourselves comfortably on the floor sitting or lying with pillows. She instructed us to close our eyes and visualize where we would like to be, walking by the ocean, sitting by a stream, or in any beautiful scene of our **choice**. She continued with seeing someone walk toward us until face to face, asking why he or she hurt us and waiting for a reply. The session continued with questions we asked ourselves, and as it ended, when she told us to open our eyes, some had been crying as she had forewarned. It was a session to confront and begin purging our pain and garbage.

I felt a little out of place because I didn't cry. I couldn't visualize a face. I saw Bud's face for a moment unable to keep his image before me.

I couldn't feel the hurt I once felt which told me that I had let go, and I couldn't see any other. I realized then that the quiet times I gave myself on an almost daily basis was a form of meditation. It was a nice discovery that I was already into meditation, using visualization or imagery and creating my own colorful and expansive scenes.

The workshop taught me to create and follow a daily meditation routine after each day's work at approximately the same time, place, and position, and always after a shower which often included hair washing as the physical and symbolic act of cleansing unwanted garbage picked up during the day. Meditation purged my garbage better than jogging, leaving me calm, refreshed without fuss or muss, and became my primary means of quieting mind, body, and spirit.

About a month after I had begun that routine, I decided to use meditation to help me lose weight. It was a thought received after watching part of a brief television message by a gentleman who told his audience to "turn down the fat thermostat" to lose weight, and though not spectacular, it stuck in my mind. The next day I thought about it and said, "Why not try it? Why not make it part of my meditation? Since I believe in taking care of the inner to take care of the outer, why not do just that to lose weight? I always stressed when dieting, so why deny myself if I want to eat it? Stressing self isn't loving, so give it a go!" I had to pick out a thermostat and what was better than a thermometer with red fluid marked with my current weight and the desired one. I hurried home to try it out.

I settled into position, took the usual three deep breaths and visualized myself walking along the beach on a lovely, sunny day, enjoying the ocean's expansive view. As I turned my head, I saw someone at a distance, walking towards me. As the figure drew closer, I saw that it was a woman, slender, carrying herself well, a picture of serenity. She stopped in front of me, and as I looked at her smiling face, I saw myself. As I gazed at her, I noted a large thermometer on the side with the red fluid slowly falling from my current weight. I hadn't picked a target weight prior to meditation but took the first number that came to mind. As I held that picture in my mind, I told myself I would lose weight no matter what I ate, wouldn't deny myself anything I wanted, including sweets, and would lean toward nutritious food. I would not state a time frame for the loss, would use Tai Chi Chuan as exercise, and would be well, look well.

That time I had a strong desire, fortified with the belief and determination, to accomplish my goal without stress. How well I remembered the many other times I had tried only to get stressed with "no, you can't have it" and gained more than I had lost. I was determined to succeed with the inner knowing which brought belief, faith, to the forefront and discipline to meditate daily. The first fifteen minutes of each session were seeing myself lose weight, a practice for six months with a gradual decrease in time spent on that picture.

More than two weeks had passed before I lost a pound followed by two more pounds in the next two weeks. I definitely was losing and decided to use loose clothes, not the scale, as my guide for weight loss because monitoring numbers would cause and perpetuate stress, like when we use time as a constraint.

As weeks passed, clothes became looser, and after about six months, it was time to shop for new clothes. It was a pleasurable activity especially when the sales staff, at first glance, said I needed a smaller size than requested.

While meditation continued daily, I decreased weight loss visions after six months to three times weekly and by the end of the year, occasionally for a couple minutes. I lost forty-two pounds in six months, resulting in a holistic sense of well-being in mind, body, and spirit. It took a little over a year to reach a satisfactory point, and although I didn't reach my visualized goal, I had lost fifty pounds, just four from my goal, another first time feat for me.

Something happened during that process. I found myself changing my food intake, consuming until satisfied, not stuffed to the max. I ate more vegetables, cooked and fresh, with grain, beans, and fruits, and cut back on beef and pork and included more poultry and seafood. I don't think I had more tossed salads for lunches than during that time, a good deterrent for snacking because chewing tired me and diminished desire for anything else. The anything else was sweets. Whenever I did want sweets, I'd ask myself, "do I *really need* it?" the answer almost always was no, but when I did want it, I treated myself. Eating out was another matter. Since it was occasional, I ate whatever I wanted, but still found the amounts and kinds diminishing. It was done without stress because I had decided from the beginning weight loss would come regardless of what I ate, and more importantly, without stress.

I maintained my weight for three years, and did regain twenty since then, but I know that, if I **choose** to lose again, I will. In retrospect, I believe that meditation was the key to my weight loss for it changed my attitude toward self. It helped release my stressed outlook, replacing it with greater calm, understanding, and acceptance to have faith and do, i.e. if I really wanted it and believed in it, that "Thot" became a "thing".

Meditation has become an invaluable lesson and a must to place me closer to God.

XIX

ALOHA

*W*hen my daughter's college graduation drew near, thoughts turned to my own future. Her graduation meant release from an emotional and financial responsibility and a beginning for travel, a desire I seemed to have had forever. I would at last be able to have that long ago "Thot" become a "thing".

Where and when? Many places and soon as possible, but first, I had to meet with all my children. It was finally my turn to have a serious talk with them, something I had planned for since they were tots. I knew that someday I would have to let them go to find their own way without almost constant worry for their welfare. The time also had come for those who clung for emotional or financial support to let go, for they too must and could stand on their own two feet. Any problems they would encounter would be their doing, and therefore their responsibility to solve. They no longer needed me.

The day my daughter began college, I knew that her graduation would culminate in the closing of the last chapter in one book and the beginning of another—a new life. On one hand, I felt sadness at the thought of closing that book, yet on the other, I wanted the freedom and looked forward with eagerness. They had been practically my whole life, and we had been through some tough ups and downs, but my future was yet to be discovered. It was time for this mother ship to pull up anchor and go sailing.

So far, my life has been a fulfilling experience of many lessons to answer many whys. It has brought forth a beginning to understand and accept others and myself without control and judgment. It has brought a learning to clear my muddy vision and see interactions and relations of many. It has brought into focus the meaning and importance of balance to attain and maintain healthful living, to live in harmony with all, and to be ever mindful of my spiritual being in a physical body.

I now see that balance includes differences in all. Without differences, I could not have learned to make **choices** and remain on this path. With my limited mind, how else could I have seen good and bad, war and peace, love and hate, night and day, and many more? It was in first seeing the difference, am now able to see the likeness or oneness of all things. In essence, all things just are, but it was my "Thots" that gave them demarcation, differences, "things", causing me confusion and uncertainty in **choosing**.

I have learned that *free will* is responsibility, not irresponsibility and that loving myself gives me the courage for risk taking. Loving myself gives me the confidence to know that all things are possible and instills the desire to continue searching for knowledge and understanding, that is, Truth. Most importantly, it gives me back to myself so I may know what living is all about and supports me to **choose**.

Love is that special light within each of us which waits to emerge and transform us into light beings. To err is human but to become better is divine—our true destiny. I see that path for all—to become as the Almighty, the Universal Source—God.

Aloha nui loa (Hawaiian for goodbye and much affection)

It's My Choice

by SM Chung

Trafford Publishing

book review by Sherokee Ilse

"I believe free will gives us a choice to enable healing of mind, body, and spirit. With it we can choose our path, crooked or straight. Choice... made with a thought which, when believed, becomes a thing."

"Talk Story," a Hawaiian phrase that promotes sharing one's life stories, is alive and well within the covers of this book. The belief that, "We all have choices which define and guide us through our lives," sets the stage for an intimate, honest journey of life stories told during the author's time in Hawaii.

After a significant loss, Chung realizes she has been living life as a victim. "What did I do to deserve this?" Soon she chooses to rely on personal choice based on self-love, faith in self and God, and a belief that she can move to a place of being a victor through being responsible and self-reliant. Narratives of parenting, working, and managing her health offer wise examples of lessons learned, such as—accepting self and others reduces stress; imposing our personal values on others doesn't make for successful living, rather, working to make ourselves better makes for better living; thinking the best of others and helping when we are able, allows us to reach oneness with the Almighty. Other lessons that strike familiar cords are woven into a lengthy and stressful workplace challenge she endured: We can control only ourselves, not others, and it doesn't pay to take advantage or intimidate another because what goes around comes around.

While the author's accounts relate to her life, they inspire others to examine their own philosophies. Many people have a lack of self-worth combined with a fear of losing their self-images and identity. Staying in the same safe place can aid to feeling victimized, misunderstood, and controlled by others. By learning to love themselves and take personal responsibility for thoughts and beliefs, success and fulfillment may follow. Positive, practical messages flow throughout the entire book, offering inspiration and hope to those who have the courage and faith to take risks and to continue to evolve.

RECOMMENDED by the US Review

* * * * * * * * *

 Pacific Book Review

helping authors succeed!

REVIEW

In this energy-based life every second of every day, we make choices, particularly by virtue of our thoughts, no matter how big or small. We consciously make a choice with our thoughts, we are responsible for our thoughts, which in turn have consequences, as a matter of fact, your thoughts become "things" or rather your thoughts manifest your reality. This premise is aptly expressed In SM Chung's recent work It's My Choice, within which she shares her experiences with making choices along her spiritual journey, which led to her self-healing.

From the outset, author Chung primarily promotes the belief that by choosing to heal ourselves through self-love, it also heals the external world around you. By making the conscious choice to heal ourselves, from the soul level, we also choose to allow it to manifest through your actions and into your reality, which in turn by healing brings balance and wholeness to you and the world around you.

Moreover, this is a prolific work ripe with spiritual truisms based on thoughtful insights garnered from author SM Chung's life borne experiences, the tangibility of which is expressed with an overview of pragmatism and honesty which readers will find resonate both in truth and in scope.

Retrospectively, Author Chung's spiritually expansive journey starts with the unexpected death of her husband, which triggered her looking more deeply into her choices. She examined her thoughts and her actions within the scenario and throughout the relationship. Consequently, as the book progresses, we share her journey with her life as a widow, mother, daughter, employee, and friend delving into how free will, expectations, and the choices made by both ourselves and others can steer our lives toward greatness or disaster.

Overall, I enjoyed the work that author Chung posits through her narrative in It's My Choice. This book made for a spiritually edifying read, worthy of adding to any metaphysical library. She presents a deeply insightful understanding of how the thoughts she chose to think in her life-borne interactions became somehow expressed within her reality, making the overall premise explored in this compelling narrative "choose your thoughts wisely because thoughts become things," a very plausible tenet of humanity's spiritual reality. Moreover, the book presents her story with a well-paced flowing narrative that readers will not become lost within the material because of unrelatable esoteric terms or wording, her story is simple to the point and well expressed, often giving insightful nuggets of worthwhile food for thought. I highly recommend this book as an addition to any library.